Y0-BCV-861

THE LAST EPISODE OF THE FRENCH REVOLUTION

BEING

A HISTORY OF GRACCHUS BABEUF AND THE CONSPIRACY OF THE EQUALS

GRACCHUS BABEUF

From an engraving in E.-F. De Saint Martin's '60 Ans d'un Peuple' (1804)

THE LAST EPISODE OF THE
FRENCH REVOLUTION

BEING A HISTORY OF

GRACCHUS BABEUF

AND THE CONSPIRACY OF THE EQUALS

BY

ERNEST BELFORT BAX

AUTHOR OF
"MARAT: THE PEOPLE'S FRIEND,"
"THE STORY OF THE FRENCH REVOLUTION,"
"THE SOCIAL SIDE OF THE REFORMATION IN GERMANY,"
ETC., ETC.

HASKELL HOUSE PUBLISHERS Ltd.
Publishers of Scarce Scholarly Books
NEW YORK. N. Y. 10012
1971

First Published 1911

HASKELL HOUSE PUBLISHERS LTD.
Publishers of Scarce Scholarly Books
280 LAFAYETTE STREET
NEW YORK, N. Y. 10012

Library of Congress Catalog Card Number: **74-159489**

Standard Book Number 8383-1282-9

Printed in the United States of America

NOTE ON AUTHORITIES

As the principal sources that have been used in the preparation of the following study may be mentioned :—

(1) The careful and exhaustive *Histoire de Gracchus Babeuf et du Babouvisme*, largely based on hitherto unpublished documents, by M. Victor Advielle. 2 vols. (Paris, 1884).

(2) *Gracchus Babeuf et le Conspiration des Egaux*, by Philippe Buonarroti (Paris, 1830), a first-hand narrative by one of the principal actors in the drama he describes.

(3) *Babeuf et le Socialisme en* 1796, par Edouard Fleury (Paris, 1851), a book preserving some interesting details, but prejudiced and not altogether reliable.

(4) Among the contemporary sources for the history of the movement, the *Copie des Pièces saisies dans le local que Babeuf occupoit lors de son arrestation* (Paris, Nivôse, Ann. V.) occupies an important place. It consists in a volume officially published by the High Court immediately after the trial, containing a complete collection of the *pièces de conviction* which formed the basis of the prosecution.

(5) The collection of the numbers of Babeuf's journals, the *Journal de la Liberté de la Presse* and the *Tribun du Peuple*, together with the few numbers of the *Éclaireur*, a journal published for a short time by Babeuf's friend Sylvain Maréchal, to be found in the Bibliothèque Nationale in Paris.

Other, minor, references are given in the text.

Allusions to, and accounts of, the movement are, of course, to be found in all the journals of the time, but they are for the most part utterly prejudiced, and contain no facts of importance not given by Buonarroti or contained in the officially published documents.

PREFACE

OF all the leading actors in the great drama of the French Revolution, there is probably none less known to the average reader of history than the subject of the present volume. All that has appeared in English in book form up to the present time consists, I believe, in Bronterre O'Brien's translation of Buonaroti's account of the Movement of the " Equals," now long since out of print. The reason for this neglect, and for the lack of interest generally shown in Babeuf, is probably in part to be looked for in the fact that Babeuf's public activity consisted of a kind of aftermath of the great historical events of the Revolution. The Revolution, properly speaking, had run its course before Babeuf appeared on the scene. The principal leaders were fallen or dispersed, the ragged levies of the people's quarters of St Antoine and St Marceau had risen *en masse* for the last time, and had been beaten and disarmed by the forces of the new governing class that had installed itself in the seats of the old royal and feudal authorities. François Noel Babeuf, the subsequent Gracchus, played no political rôle of any importance while the Revolution was at its zenith. His name became first prominent in the year IV. (1795), when the Society, which later on met near the Pantheon, was formed. The usual fate of secret movements, of conspiracies, overtook Babeuf's. It was killed by treachery—killed, as its promoters fondly believed, on the eve of success. In a word, the movement was a failure, and its memory with the great world soon tended to pass into oblivion. Nevertheless, for students of the earlier democratic movements, and of the precursors of modern Socialism, the agitation of Babeuf in the last decade of the eighteenth century must be of keen interest.

I may mention that the following monograph represents the carrying out of a wish, expressed some years before he died, of my old friend, William Morris, who thought that a clear and concise account of the Babeuf incident in English was wanted, and who urged me to undertake the task. Whether this little volume answers the requirements of the case must be left for the reader to judge.

E. B. B.

CONTENTS

ERRATA

Page 21, line 10 from top, for *former* read *latter*.

Page 40, line 7 from top, for *Rousin* read *Ronsin*.

Page 86, line 13 from bottom, insert comma after *issued*.

Page 104, line 4 from top, for *arrest* read *his attempted arrest*.

Page 195, top line, delete *those of.*

INTRODUCTION

To understand the history and the real significance
of even the most prominent ideas of an epoch, it is
necessary to realise what constitutes the mental
background, as we may term it, of the period in
question, for it is this that gives to the expressed
ideas of a time their real significance.   It has often
been remarked that the same actual words or
phrases may have a different meaning at different
times.   To take a familiar illustration—that of Dr
Johnson's well-known aphorism that " patriotism is
the last resort of scoundrels."   The uneducated or
half-educated man in the street of to-day would
regard this *mot* as an attack by some " little
Englander " on the Jingo or Imperialist with whom
he is familiar,—the background of his mind, in the
light of which he interprets it, consisting of the
conditions of English politics that have grown up
during the last generation.   Needless to say, the
expression to the mind of Dr Johnson, who first
used it, had an entirely different, and in some

respects even an opposite, meaning. He knew nothing of modern Imperialism, of the glorious British Empire upon which the sun never sets: what was in his mind was the antithesis, not between the advocate of an aggressive British Empire and a respecter of the rights of weaker peoples, but an advocate of the rights of the people of a given country against its ruling classes. This was the sense in which the eighteenth century, for the most part, understood the words " patriot " and " patriotism," the great political antithesis of the eighteenth century being that between rulers and people. This is an obvious instance. But the capacity of the same form of words to express totally different meanings according to the age in which they appear, and the great danger of their entire falsification by reading into them the mind of a later period, can never be sufficiently present to the sense of the historian. Every form of ideas that belongs to a past period of history, no matter how modern it may look, we may be quite sure is not what it appears to us of the twentieth century at first sight. The intellectual background of the men who enunciated the ideas in question is so different, that the meaning present to them in the expressions used and the meaning they evoke in us cannot possibly be the same.

The above remarks apply to our estimation of eighteenth century thought generally, and, not least,

to the thought of the French Revolution. To
understand this thought properly, we have to
investigate the conditions that reflected themselves
in the mental background of the leading actors.
One thing we have to do is to eliminate all concep-
tions having their origin in the doctrine of evolution
from their mental framework. This it is somewhat
difficult for the present generation effectually to
accomplish. Our whole thought is so bound up
with the notion of development, that it is difficult
for us to realise the intellectual attitude of the man
of intelligence to whom this idea has never presented
itself. Yet, needless to say, to the eighteenth-
century thinker in general it was entirely absent.
Very noticeable is this in the theories of society
prevalent during the eighteenth century, and that
formed the groundwork of the thought of the
French Revolution. The main principle upon
which it all turned was that of conscious and
arbitrary construction. Society, as it existed, was
conceived as the outcome of a contract made in
remote ages, and which might be unmade or altered
at the will of its individual members at any time.
The classics still bulked largely in the cultured
man's outlook on history, politics, and the world in
general. In seventeenth-century England this
was modified by the place the English Bible held
in the imagination of all classes. Hence in the
British political struggles of the seventeenth century

we find the Old Testament the great storehouse
of instances on which the popular imagination falls
back.   In France of the eighteenth century, on the
contrary, the classical tradition held undisturbed
sway, alike with the cultivated and the popular
intelligence. The very names indicate this.   In
the place of Biblical names we have Anacharsis
Clootz, Anaxagoras Chaumette, Gracchus Babeuf,
and the like.   Everyone with the smallest smatter-
ing of education talked Roman History, just as in
the English political movements of the preceding
century everyone talked Old Testament.   As for
the literary movement in France, this was derived
mainly from English sources.   Hobbes, Locke,
Shaftesbury, Hutcheson, Mandeville, Bolingbroke,
and other less known English writers contributed
to build up the theories of Condillac, Helvetius,
D'Holbach, Voltaire, Rousseau, and the Encyclo-
pædists.

Political and social ideas of the time were naturally dominated by the leading political forms of
the seventeenth and eighteenth centuries. These
were absolutism, working through a bureaucracy,
on the one side, and an all but rightless people,
composed more or less of a downtrodden peasantry
in the country, and a middle-class, still largely
composed of small masters, in the towns.   A proletariat in the modern sense, which implies the
existence of the great machine-industry, did not

exist. But a population, not as yet relatively very numerous except in a few large towns, of journeymen and labourers, which was destined to become the groundwork of the modern proletariat, did undoubtedly obtain, but obtained only as an economic appendix of the small middle-class to which reference has been made. The old feudal landowning class, which had come down from mediæval times, had now in the main become an absentee landowning class, dancing attendance at courts and growing financially poorer. While still retaining many of its feudal privileges, it functioned for the most part through its members holding positions in the bureaucratic hierarchy which centred in the Crown. As a consequence of the foregoing conditions, the leading political category of the seventeenth and eighteenth centuries was that of Ruler and Subject. Similarly, the leading economic category was that of Rich and Poor. It may be said, of course, that these categories obtain also to-day. But they are no longer dominant as categories in their bare abstractness, as they were in the eighteenth century. In the Western Europe of modern times absolutism has uniformly broken down in favour of some form of popular representation. Hence there is, in theory at least, no longer a pure and unadulterated Ruler in the old sense, any more than there is a pure and unadulterated Subject in the old sense. In a word, with the dominance in the political sphere of some form of Constitutionalism, the edge of the old antithesis has become blunted. It has no longer, in its old and bare form, the incisive force that it once had.

Again, the corresponding leading antithesis of the eighteenth century in economics, that of Rich and Poor, has likewise in a measure lost its pregnancy in the modern world. The rich are no longer an approximately homogeneous class over against the poor, as also a relatively homogeneous section of society. There is no one class of rich men more or less completely dominating the economic situation of to-day, as did the French noble and higher ecclesiastic of the *ancien régime*. In the most recent developments of modern Capitalism, it is true that the financial Capitalist takes the lead. But he does not, as yet, completely dominate the economic situation. The Industrial Capitalist or Syndicate plays a scarcely less important part in the economic system of the modern world, while the old Landowner, who has come down from the ages of feudalism, still continues to exist, even if he no longer flourishes as of yore. The interests, moreover, of the Landowner as such, and of the Industrial Capitalist as such, are often in strong conflict. The same may be said of the small Capitalist and of the large Capitalist. In fact, the Capitalist class itself is not homogeneous. If there is no homogeneous rich class to-day, there is certainly no homogeneous poor class: the small middle-class is more or less decadent. The " Poor," like the " People," is, in short, an expression covering various distinct social groups to-day, with aims and interests by no means always harmonious, not to say identical. To-day the economic antithesis receives its most adequate expression, not in the vague and more or less amorphous concepts of " Rich " and " Poor," but in the extreme poles of the antithesis, that of Capitalist on the one hand and Workman on the other.

The Capitalist System, which forms the economic basis of present society, points more and more to the possessor or effective controller of the means of production, on the one hand, and the workman who has nought but his labour power, on the other, as representing the salient economic antithesis of the world in which we live. It is, if one will, of course only a mode of the old time-honoured antithesis of Rich and Poor, but its importance consists in the fact that it is a mode which defines the relation with regard to contemporary conditions which the old, vague antithesis of Rich and Poor does not do. The latter sufficed for a time when the class conflicts of the modern world were in embryo, when the modern Proletariat, with its economic complement, the great Industrial Bourgeoisie, was in its infancy.

At that time the working classes of the towns, taking them in the bulk, were not yet readily distinguishable, as regards their interests, from the poorer sections of the middle-class. The whole question seemed only one of degree, from the well-to-do (for that time) large employer of labour like Reveillon or Santerre, a *rara avis*, of whom only a few specimens existed in Paris and in other large towns, through the small master working himself and employing a few journeymen to assist him, to the small independent craftsman who could not afford to employ labour, down to the journeyman labourer himself. There seemed no essential economic halting-place. At the top of the scale you had a man relatively rich, but still not rich as the noble was rich, and at the lower end of the scale you had various gradations of poverty. Outside this small industrial middle-class of the towns was to be found the man of the land, the peasant, who formed the bulk of the population of France. Here, in the peasant in his hut, as against the noble in his château, the lord of the countryside, was to be found the antithesis of rich and poor in its most direct and its sharpest form. Bad seasons and abject local conditions had driven numbers of the peasantry into the towns, both before and during the early years of the Revolution. These detached elements of the rural class formed a vagabond population, living from hand to mouth, and not fitting into any distinct

section of society as then organised. In the France
of the eighteenth century, the intellectual and
bureaucratic middle-class, including the middle
ranks of the clergy, attached by social and economic
bonds to the smaller noblesse, and which formed
the intellectual backbone of the moderate side of
the Revolution, are not to be confounded, it should
be observed, with the industrial middle-class.
Though also men of the Third Estate, they must
not be identified with the former. From them the
ranks of the Constitutionalists and Girondists were
mainly recruited.

From what has been said, it will be evident how
the appeals of Babeuf and those who thought like
him were necessarily to the poor in general, unlike
the appeal of the modern Socialist agitation, which
is pre-eminently to the working-classes of the great
industry—to the modern proletariat. Similarly,
from the political side, the appeal of the French
Revolutionist was to man in general. He called
upon him to claim his rights as citizen. The appeal
of the modern Socialist is not so much to man in
general, to man in the abstract, as to man as the
producer of wealth; in other words, to the workman.
He, the Socialist, calls upon the workman, as the
producer of wealth, to claim his right as a class, to
be at once possessor, controller, and organiser of
production and the enjoyer of the wealth produced.
The idea of citizenship is not sufficiently definite for

modern use.   All these considerations are necessary
to be taken into account in judging the outlook of
the men of the Revolution.   Their sociological and
political prospective was abstract.   They regarded
all things as dominated by abstractions—right,
virtue, citizenship, man.

Even the great Revolutionary trinity, " Liberty,
Equality, Fraternity," was conceived of in the
abstract way of looking at things peculiar to the
eighteenth century.   In the absence of the idea
of evolution it was inevitable that society should
be regarded as governed by such abstract notions.
Modern Socialist thought, on the other hand,
seeks a realisation of " Liberty, Equality, and
Fraternity " in the concrete development of a
new society from germs present in existing society.
It takes its stand upon a social growth—economical, political, and ethical—which has in the
past proceeded, in the main, independently of
the conscious will of man.   To the eighteenth
century, liberty was a formal pattern, to be applied
as a label is applied in the most superficial
manner.   The modern mind sees that often-
times a formal liberty, such as that, for example,
comprised in so-called " liberty of contract " as
between the possessor of the means of production
and the propertyless workman, is a mere form and
nothing more—a form concealing a content which
is its very opposite.   It is seen clearly by the modern

revolutionary thinker that the superficial form of any idea may easily be only a blind, and that what we have to look to is its concrete embodiment in a given society. To this more than a mere label is necessary. The Paris of the French Revolution was enamoured of the bare word "liberty," and felt it a revolutionary duty to apply it on every occasion and in every detail of life in its barest form, so that the Parisians of 1793 opened all the cages of their song-birds and let the inmates fly away, with the result that the streets of Paris were strewn with the dead bodies of canaries and other hapless victims. This is a trivial illustration of devotion to a term applied in its hard, formal abstraction, or as a label.

We are not free even in the present day from the worship of an abstract phrase connoting an idea regardless of its real content. This is very noticeable in the modern Feminist movement. We find the notion of chivalry, as implying consideration and deference for weakness, exploited to its fullest extent by the Feminist advocate, by using the notion of weakness as a superficial label applied to every member of the female sex, regardless of the facts or circumstances of any given case, or of the general social conditions obtaining to-day. As a matter of fact, the physical strength or weakness of the individual counts for very little in the present age, when disputes are decided, not by personal prowess, but by the power of the State, through its accredited organs. A woman in the power of the law or opposed by superior force could under no circumstances be in worse case than a man similarly situated. But the fact is, by virtue of this very sex weakness she is in a much stronger position than the man, and hence deserves much less pity than a man would do under like circumstances. A maudlin sentiment is sought to be aroused in the public mind by the employment of the notions of weakness and chivalry as the label, the justification for which is purely formal and abstract, and which is contradicted by the content of every given case, as determined by existing law and public opinion. Formal sex weakness and disability has thus been converted into real sex strength and domination. But by dint of ignoring this conversion, and taking his stand on physiological facts which under modern conditions have become purely irrelevant, the feminist can succeed in hoodwinking public opinion as to the reality embodied in the facts, and hence as to the true distribution of effective strength and weakness between the sexes in modern society.

Though the course of the French Revolution, up to the time of Gracchus Babeuf's entry into the political arena, is one of those matters with which every modern representative of Macaulay's Schoolboy is supposed to be familiar, it may not be out of place for those readers whose Revolution lore is not altogether as fresh as it might be to devote a few pages to a short sketch of the course of events from the assembly of the States-General on May the 5th, 1789, to the Revolution of the 9th of Thermidor, July the 27th, 1794, consequent on which the political activity proper of Babeuf began.

The day after the opening of the States-General was signalised by the insistence of the Third Estate on its being joined by the other Estates in the large hall of Versailles. Wrangling as to the form the deliberations should take—the First and Second Estates, *i.e.* the nobility and higher clergy, with few exceptions, refusing to unite in the same council chamber with the Third Estate—continued till June the 15th, when, on the proposal of the Abbé Siéyès, the Third Estate proclaimed itself the representative assembly of the French nation. The title of National Assembly was adopted the next day. This action was followed on the 20th of the month by the closing of the great hall by the king and the adjournment of the Constituent National Assembly to the Tennis Court, where the famous oath was taken not to separate till a constitution had been given to France. The king in vain attempted to annul the action of the Third Estate, and finally, after some days, agreed to the union of the Estates as a National Assembly.

On the 11th of July the king refused to accede to the Assembly's request to remove the troops then at Versailles, and at the same time dismissed the popular minister, Necker. The latter event aroused the whole of Paris, and was followed by meetings and tumults throughout the city. The next day a citizen guard was formed in Paris sixty thousand strong, pikes were forged and guns sought for. On the 14th, in the belief that a royal attack on the city from Versailles was imminent, the search for arms was redoubled, the Bastille was stormed and taken.

Emigration of nobles now began on a large scale, and at the same time the burning of châteaux went on throughout the countryside. On the celebrated night of the 4th of August the Assembly abolished all feudal rights, and established equality before the law and personal liberty, by decree. Within the next few days the lands and buildings of the Church were in principle declared national property. Necker, who had been recalled by the king after the taking of the Bastille, towards the end of September made vigorous but abortive attempts to raise by loan sufficient money to meet the situation.

Meanwhile starvation and want made fearful havoc in Paris, till on October the 5th several thousand women, followed by immense crowds, marched to Versailles, Lafayette following later on

with his National Guards. The Assembly and the
royal palace were invaded by the populace, the
majority of whom remained in Versailles throughout the night, renewing the attack on the palace
the following day. The upshot of the whole affair
was that on the afternoon of October 6th the royal
family were forced to follow the crowd to Paris,
taking up their residence in the Tuileries. The
Assembly soon transferred itself also to Paris,
where it continued its work of building up the
constitution.

The map of France was now altered, the old
provinces abolished, and their place taken by eighty-
three departments, with corresponding administra-
tive bodies. The old parliaments were abolished
and new law courts established. The civil constitution of the clergy was now completed and promulgated. On November the 3rd the Assembly
formally confiscated the effects of the clergy,
abolishing them as a separate order.

About this time the Jacobin Club, so called
from its meeting in the old Jacobin convent in the
Rue St Honoré, began to exercise an important
influence in public affairs. The work of feder-
ating the newly organised French nation in its
new districts and departments now went on apace,
but all the time plots were being hatched to get
the king away to Metz, there to place himself at
the head of an army that had been formed by the

emigrant aristocrats.   Some of the principal of
these nobles were maintained at Trier, Turin, and
other places in the neighbourhood of the French
frontiers by the Court.   The ecclesiastical estates
were now sold, and served as the security for the
new issue of paper money (*assignats*) inaugurated
by Necker.   On the 14th of July of this year, 1790,
the anniversary of the taking of the Bastille, a great
festival of the Federation of all France was held in
Paris, on the Champs de Mars.   Soon after this,
fresh clubs sprang up in all directions, which became
affiliated to the Jacobin Society of Paris.   In Paris
itself, the Club of the Cordeliers, which embraced
Danton, Marat, and Hébert, was founded as a more
democratic rival of the Jacobins.

In August occurred the famous affair of Nancy,
which began by an outrage offered to two envoys
of a Swiss regiment by French officers.   This Swiss
regiment became popular with French revolutionists
everywhere.   Bouillé, the commander of the troops
on the eastern frontier, ordered the Swiss to evacuate
Nancy, where they were quartered.   They refused,
with the result that Bouillé, with the aid of some
German regiments and seven hundred royalist
guards, ordered a massacre, in which half of the
Swiss regiment fell, after which twenty-one were
hanged and fifty sent to the galleys.   This affair
of the " Nancy massacre," as it was called, was an
epoch-making event, fraught with important con-

sequences to the **Revolution**. Henceforward the Assembly, which had played an equivocal rôle in the whole business, together with the king condoning Bouillé's crime, became more and more distrusted by the popular party. The clubs developed an extraordinary activity, and rose to be of paramount importance in the political life of Paris and of France.

Early in September, soon after the news of the Nancy massacre arrived in Paris, Necker escaped from Paris and France, having become unpopular, and impossible any longer as Finance Minister. In January the clergy in the Assembly were challenged to take the oath to the Constitution. Many of them refused, thereby exacerbating the situation. On April the 2nd, Mirabeau, the most powerful mediating force between the old and the new régimes, died. This left an opening for the influence of Robespierre and other leaders of the Jacobin and Cordelier Clubs.

On the night of the 20th of June the famous attempted flight of the king took place, the idea being that Louis, together with his family, was to be received by Bouillé on the eastern frontier, prior to the latter marching on Paris with his army to suppress the Revolution. The king, as is well known, was recognised by the ex-dragoon and postmaster Drouet, who apprised the authorities at Varennes, the next town at which the royal

party would have to change horses, with the result
that Louis and his belongings were brought back
to Paris.   Henceforward the popular party was
becoming more and more republican.   The moderate party in the Assembly succeeded in getting
the king reinstated after his virtual abdication,
under conditions, which did not, however, satisfy
the popular party, the latter demanding his
summary dethronement, if not the establishment
of a Republic.   A gigantic petition to this effect,
and claiming that the matter should be brought
before the nation, was carried to the Champs de
Mars by an immense crowd on July the 17th of
this year (1791).   Lafayette, accompanied by the
mayor of Paris, Bailly, arrived on the ground at
the head of a force of the National Guard : result,
the notorious massacre of the Champs de Mars.
This event produced consternation in the ranks of
the popular party, and a temporary check to the
Revolutionary movement.

At the end of September the Constituent
Assembly, which, as we have seen, consisted of
the members of the States-General elected in 1789,
was dissolved.   The newly elected Chamber, called
the Legislative Assembly, met on the 1st of
October.   In this second parliament the party
called at the time Brissotins, from their leader
Brissot, but known subsequently by the name of
Girondins, from the department of the Gironde,

from which many of their chief orators came, was in the ascendancy. Pétion became mayor of Paris. Meanwhile the king vetoed various decrees passed by the Assembly. At the same time he was compelled formally to remonstrate to the central European Powers for harbouring and encouraging the *émigrés* who held a kind of court at Coblentz, and whose agents were active throughout Europe in their avowed intention of invading France at the first opportunity to restore the absolute monarchy. France remained in a state of seething discontent throughout the ensuing winter, and the relations with foreign powers were to the last degree strained.

Finally, in March 1792, Louis was forced to appoint a Girondin ministry, which promptly demanded explanations from the Austrian Court. The upshot was a kind of ultimatum on the part of the emperor, demanding a return to the *ancien régime*, including the restoration of Church property, and the cession of Alsace to the German princes.

War was at last declared on the 20th of April, on the proposition of the king, who hoped for a successful invasion of the country, resulting in the restoration of his own power, and also by this means to drain off into the army to a large extent the revolutionary elements of the home population. The declaration of war was greeted with enthusiasm in Paris, as affording a relief from the tension of the previous months. The French forces consisted of three armies—the army of the north under Richambeau, the army of the centre under Lafayette, and the army of the Rhine under Luckner. The war began by an unsuccessful invasion of Brabant. The Jacobins accused the counter-revolutionaries generally of plotting for the defeat of the French armies, and the officers of treachery. On June the 28th the Assembly decreed the formation of a military camp before Paris. This decree, together with another concerning the priests who refused to take the oath of loyalty to the constitution, Louis peremptorily vetoed.

On the 20th of June an insurrectionary movement took place in Paris, the populace breaking into the Tuileries. From this time the movement for the deposition of Louis and the abolition of the monarchy gained by leaps and bounds every day. On June the 28th, Lafayette, having left his army, appeared in Paris to demand the suppression and punishment of the Jacobin party for the riot of the 20th. He obtained no favourable hearing from anyone, and returned discomfited to his army, which he not long afterwards deserted, fleeing across the frontier.

Throughout France now the enrolling of volunteers went on; numbers of these came to Paris,

ostensibly for the festival of the 14th of July. On
the 22nd of July the country was declared in danger;
the enrolment of volunteers received a double im-
petus. Recruits from the provinces arrived daily in
Paris. The Paris wardships or sections declared
themselves in permanent session. On the 25th,
Brunswick launched his famous manifesto from
Coblentz, and started on the march to Paris. Some
members of the newly enrolled Federal guards
formed a permanent committee at the Jacobins,
while the forty-eight sections of the city appointed
a central committee from their number to sit in
the Hôtel de Ville. On the 29th a newly created
battalion of guards from Marseilles arrived in Paris,
singing its war hymn, subsequently known as the
Marseillaise. The demands for the dethronement
of the king, by the Jacobin and popular party
generally, became more clamorous and insistent
than ever. Finally, on the 9th of August, a general
assembly of the sections took place at the Hôtel
de Ville, at which it was agreed to demand the
immediate abdication of the king, failing which, it
was resolved to storm the palace of the Tuileries
at midnight. The old municipal council, with its
mayor, was then declared dissolved, and its place
taken by a Revolutionary Commune.

The attack on the Tuileries took place actually
in the early morning of the 10th of August, with
the result that is well known. Louis was sub-

3

sequently imprisoned with his family in the
Temple, under the orders of the Revolutionary
Commune. By the end of August news of the
clerical and royalist outbreak in La Vendée reached
Paris. The arrest of supposed royalist plotters
within the capital took place wholesale. From
the 3rd to the 6th of September the so-called
September massacres were enacted by a body of
persons between two and three hundred strong,
who went from prison to prison killing supposed
traitors. At about the same time Dumouriez, at
the head of the raw levies of volunteers recently
formed, drove back from the wooded ridges of the
Argonne the armies of Brunswick. A week or
two later a decisive victory of the French at
Valmy relieved the situation.

The old Legislative Assembly having been dissolved, and a National Convention convoked on
a basis of universal but indirect suffrage, the
new legislative body opened its sittings on
September the 21st. The dethronement of the
king and the establishment of a Republic was
immediately decreed. A committee to draw
up the basis of a new constitution, founded on
the sovereignty of the people, was nominated.
Within the Convention, two distinct parties formed
themselves, the old Girondist party reinforced,
and the popular party, representing mainly the
Paris deputies, called the Mountain, from the fact

of its members sitting on the highest benches of the place of assembly. Outside these two parties were the mass of members called the Plain, or, in derision, the Marsh. The latter usually voted with the party which was for the time being in power. The famine in Paris, especially the scarcity of bread, now assumed serious proportions; bread riots were of daily occurrence. Within the Convention, exacerbation of parties grew daily more acute. The special *bête noire* of the Girondists was Marat, but they also dreaded Robespierre, as aiming at the Dictatorship. After weeks of wrangling, Louis was finally judged by the Convention and condemned to death without delay. On the 21st of January 1793 his execution took place on the Place de la Revolution, formerly Place Royale.

After the king's death the feud between the Mountain and the Gironde grew more bitter. The Girondists, claiming to represent the provinces as against Paris, the stronghold of the Mountain, favoured a federal republic; the Mountain, on the other hand, insisted on an united and centralised republic, dominated by Paris. The large towns of the departments favoured the federal idea, and hence its exponents, the Girondists, while Paris remained faithful to the Mountain. Up to this time the executive power had, in the main, continued uninterruptedly in the hands of the

Girondins. But the disasters now overtaking Dumouriez, the favourite general of the party, in his attempt to invade Holland, cast a suspicion of treachery, not only upon Dumouriez himself, but more or less affected the whole Girondist faction in the popular mind. Demands were made on various sides for the arrest and expulsion of twenty-two of the leading Girondists. In March, forty-four thousand communes throughout France now each appointed its permanent revolutionary committee to watch affairs, and especially to arrest and imprison suspected traitors and reactionaries.

The Girondists now succeeded in getting a commission appointed to inquire into alleged plots of the Jacobins and the popular party generally. They also obtained the indictment of Marat on a charge of inciting to disorder and breaches of the peace. Marat was tried, but triumphantly acquitted. These measures did not serve their authors, the Girondins, in any way, but merely helped to irritate their opponents. The rage of Paris, the Mountain, and the Jacobins against the party hitherto dominant in the Convention reached its climax in the last days of May, when the Commune took the lead in a popular insurrection against the Convention and the authorities. This ended on the 2nd of June in the arrest of twenty-two of the Girondist deputies, two ministers, and of the hated Commission of Twelve. The only hope for the Girondist faction lay now in the raising of the departments against what was represented as the dictatorship of Paris.

On the 14th of July, Charlotte Corday, egged on by Girondist misrepresentation, murdered Marat. The effect of this event throughout the country was immense. It roused the indignation of the whole of revolutionary France, vastly strengthening the position of the Mountain and the Jacobins. Up to this time the situation of the Girondists was not unfavourable. The chances of the Girondists' insurrection seemed by no means hopeless. They had the bulk of the provinces with them, including the large cities of the south. But before the end of July the Girondist army melted away without having struck a blow. The cities Lyons, Bordeaux, Marseilles, Caen, etc., that still adhered to the Girondist cause, were taken by the National Forces of the Republic, and for the most part paid heavily for their partisanship. Meanwhile the committee for drawing up the new constitution had finished its labours. The draft was submitted to the forty-four thousand communes of France, and accepted by an enormous majority. On the 10th of August, the anniversary of the taking of the Tuileries, the constitution was promulgated in Paris with great rejoicings. This was the famous Constitution of 1793, which became the political sheet-anchor of the French democracy. Soon after the revolution which had placed the Mountain in power, the recently formed and now strengthened executive body, the Committee of Public Safety, had decided that a democratic constitution in accordance with the views of the Jacobins should be drawn up. The task of doing this was entrusted to a prominent member of the Convention, the ex-noble and friend of Danton, Hérault de Sèchelles. He was assisted by four other Montagnards—St Just, Couthon, Ramel, and Mathieu. His draft was adopted by the Convention on June the 10th. It may be remarked that the question of the constitution had been prominently before the Convention, and more than one draft had been made by the Girondists, which had been received coldly by the Convention and public opinion, and actively opposed by the Mountain. The constitution of Hérault de Sèchelles and his colleagues, called the Constitution of 1793, was the first and only constitution emanating officially from the Mountain and the Jacobins. This constitution, though adopted, as stated, by an enormous majority of the French people through their primary assemblies, was suspended immediately after it was promulgated, and never became operative.

Invasion now threatened France from all sides. It was in August 1793 that the two committees, that of Public Safety, sometimes called the Committee of Government, and that of General Security, concerned mainly with the executive functions of police, respectively, were given largely increased powers, amounting practically to those of a dictatorship. Superhuman efforts were now made to raise and equip more troops; everywhere were enlistments and requisitions. The Republic has been adequately described as presenting, in this autumn of 1793, the appearance of an armed camp. It was now that the "Reign of Terror" began in earnest. The Committee of Public Safety declared that the Republic was revolutionary, and must remain so until all danger from the enemy was past. The incriminated Girondists were tried before the Revolutionary Tribunal and guillotined. The rest of the party were either imprisoned or outlawed. Marie Antoinette, generals, ex-deputies of the constituent and legislative assemblies, nobles, and officials of the *ancien régime* fell beneath the national knife, now in daily operation.

In October 1793 the revolutionary government was proclaimed, the dictatorship of the Committee of Public Safety came into full force, and with it the power of its now strongest member, Robespierre. The Committee of Public Safety being installed as, *de jure*, the supreme authority in France, it found that it had to make up its account with the *de facto* authority of the day, to wit, the Paris Commune. At first it was the Commune that effectively dominated the situation. Chaumette and Hébert had just instituted the worship of Reason on the ruins of Catholicism. The Commune, by means of its revolutionary army, consisting of six or seven thousand men under the command of Rousin, the dramatic author, undertook the purification of the provinces from reactionary elements, although its immediate action was mainly confined to the departments around Paris. But throughout France at this time guillotining was going on. Carrier was sent to Nantes; Lebon to Arras; Maignet, Fouché, Barras, Fréron were despatched to the cities of the south; and everywhere the revolutionary committees were active in hunting down traitors or supposed traitors.

By the end of 1793 fourteen armies were in the field. The year closed amid the success of the French arms everywhere. Friction, however, between the two rival central powers, the Committee of Public Safety and the Paris Commune, had already begun. The attack on the Paris Commune, or the Hébertist faction, as it was now called, from Hébert, one of its chief members and editor of the *Père Duchesne* journal, by the followers of Robespierre, was started by Robespierre himself on September the 5th. But the Commune was still strong. In October it inaugurated the new

worship of Reason.   Robespierre's determination
to crush the rival power was now formed.   At the
same time, within the Convention, the Mountain
was, however, showing signs of getting out of hand.
Two members, who expressed the view that the
committees were terrorising over the Convention,
were arrested and imprisoned in consequence.   In
the provinces the representatives "on mission"
dominated the situation, acting in many cases as
local dictators.

The friction between the Committee of Public
Safety, whose soul was Robespierre, and the
Commune of Paris, led by Chaumette and Hébert,
continued throughout the early part of 1794.   Of
the two chief clubs, the Jacobins and the Cordeliers,
the stronghold of Robespierre and his Committee
was the Jacobins; that of the Commune, *i.e.* of
Hébert and his followers, was the Cordeliers.
But there was a third party already in the field.
Danton and his friends had been for some time
past "lying low."   Danton himself had been away
at his home at Arcis, whence he was recalled by
his political associates.   The latter, with the
approval of their leader, started a journal vehemently hostile to the Hébertists and the Terror,
which was edited and mostly written by Camille
Desmoulins.   It was called *Le vieux Cordelier*, in
allusion to the Cordeliers Club in the old days when
Danton was its moving spirit.   In their campaign

against the Terror, the Dantonists hoped to find support in the Convention, but, as events proved, they were relying on a broken reed. Robespierre and his party had now two enemies to contend with. On the one hand he had the *Enragés*, as they were termed, namely, the Hébertists, and on the other the Pacivists, that is, Danton and his friends. It was not part of Robespierre's purpose, or that of his committee, to relax the Terror at this moment. On the other hand, Robespierre was much concerned that the handling of the system of the Terror should not get into the control of his Extremist enemies on the opposite side.

Early in March matters reached a climax. One or other of the two rival powers had to succumb. The only course for the Hébertists and the Cordeliers lay in a successful insurrection, which would break the power of the committee and of Robespierre. The beginnings of an attempt were made, but miscarried. A panic seemed to seize the Cordeliers, and no more active measures were taken. Robespierre had now the upper hand, and lost no time in having the leaders of the " Hébertist faction " arrested and dragged before the Revolutionary Tribunal, there to be charged with conspiring to destroy the Revolution by discrediting it through the excesses of their doctrines and policy.

Accordingly, on March the 24th, the leaders of the Extremist party, Hébert, Ronsin, and **Momoro**, with others, went to the guillotine, Chaumette following a few days later. The revolutionary army was disbanded, and the Commune reorganised and filled with the creatures of Robespierre. Having crushed his Extremist rivals, it only remained for Robespierre to destroy his Moderate foes. This followed with little delay. On March the 30th, Desmoulins, Philippeaux, and Westermann, with other friends of Danton, were arrested. Danton himself in vain attempted to get a hearing in the Convention, Robespierre effectually succeeding in closing his mouth. On April the 3rd he, together with the members of his party, was brought before the Revolutionary Tribunal, where he defended himself with such vigour that Robespierre had to extort a decree from the Convention depriving the accused of the right of speech. Two days later Danton and the remaining Dantonists were sent to the guillotine.

The power of Robespierre was now supreme. His next thought was the foundation of a deistic cult, of which he himself was to be the sovereign pontiff, as a counterblast to the atheistic worship of Reason inaugurated by the Hébertists. The Convention obediently voted his instructions in this respect, and the Festival of the Supreme Being was held on June the 8th, 1794, in the Tuileries gardens, the principal features of the ceremony being an oration from the high-priest

Robespierre, following which he set fire to certain stage-property figures constructed to represent atheism and other doctrines of the Hébertists that he disliked. The Convention, which at Robespierre's behest had shortly before decreed the existence of a Supreme Being and the immortality of the soul, was, two days after the festival in honour of these dogmas, called upon by the same dictator to pass the celebrated law of *Prairial*, which enacted that no prisoner haled before the Revolutionary Tribunal should have the right of any defence whatever.

The next weeks saw a frightful increase in the activity of the guillotine, which every day received its holocausts. But at the same time an undercurrent of fear and detestation and indeterminate revolt was rising higher and higher every day. Meanwhile, on the 26th June, the battle of Fleurus was won by General Jourdan, and the enemy driven from the Austrian Netherlands. Thus was France freed from danger, and the last point of her threatened frontiers relieved. The imminent danger of a foreign invasion was now definitely conjured, and therewith the main excuse for the institution of the " Terror " crumbled to pieces. But nevertheless the Terror continued.

At last the reckoning came. It was on the 9th of Thermidor (27th of July) 1794. Robespierre, feeling himself with his little group of satellites daily becoming more and more isolated amid the hatred and imperfectly suppressed revolt of Convention and committee men, on the 8th of Thermidor (July the 26th) appeared in the Convention after a long absence, with a violent and threatening speech, demanding powers to purge the Convention and the committees alike. This, after a moment's hesitation on the part of the Convention, started the open revolt against the Robespierrian dictatorship. At the sitting of the following day, Robespierre and his partisans, including his brother, Couthon, St Just, and Lebas, were decreed accused. In the early morning of the 28th, Robespierre and his partisans were surrounded in the Hôtel de Ville. At four o'clock in the afternoon Robespierre himself and the other chiefs of the Robespierrian faction fell beneath the guillotine. Thus ended the celebrated revolution of the 9th of Thermidor (27th of July), year II. (1794). The immediate upshot was the end of the system of the Terror, soon followed by serious modifications in the public authorities. Various economic measures passed by the Convention to relieve distress, among them the Law of Maximum, were repealed during the ensuing months. The Jacobin Club was closed in November, and the Convention began steadily and unmistakably to enter the pathway of reaction.

It was now, during this autumn of 1794, that the great political activity of Gracchus Babeuf in

Paris began, and began in the sense of the Thermidoreans, as the makers of the recent revolution were termed. The earlier period of his Paris journalism was signalised, as the reader will see, by vehement attacks on the fallen *régime* of the Terror and all connected with it. His subsequent change of opinions in this connection must be directly attributed to the reactionary character assumed by the new government, which was manned by Thermidoreans, and by the Convention itself, dominated, as it was, by the members of the same party and other reactionary elements, such as the remnants of the Girondin faction which were allowed to regain possession of their seats in the national legislature. With his growing bitterness towards the new authorities and the daily increasing reaction generally, moreover, grew Babeuf's clearness of vision as to the ends he ultimately had in view. The Constitution of 1793, and the other political objects for which he strove, he now regarded merely as a means towards a communistic state of society, which was necessarily conceived by him under the only guise possible for a man of the eighteenth century to envisage it.

CHAPTER I

FRANÇOIS NOEL BABEUF, it has now been decided
by the researches of M. Victor Advielle, was born at
St Quentin, on Sunday the 23rd November 1760.
Babeuf, in some of the *notes intimes* which the
industry of the same investigator has unearthed,
states, that he was born of so delicate a constitution that he was not expected to live. This he
attributes to the poor circumstances of his parents,
and the privations of his mother during her pregnancy. Babeuf's father appears to have been
many years older than his mother. The former is
described in the certificate of birth as "employé
des fermes du roy au Faubourg St Martin de la
ville de St Quentin," of which town his mother
was also a native. There is little doubt, however,
that they originally came from the small town of
Bobeuf, or Babœuf, in Picardy, in the present
department of the Oise. This commune is stated
to have been founded by a descendant of the
family of Calvin, to have been peopled by a colony

of Protestant refugees from various quarters, and to have maintained relations with other similar Calvinist colonies, all composed of peasant cultivators.

It is related of Babeuf's father that, on account of his abilities, he was in his younger days deputed by the members of the colony to undertake some negotiations in various foreign countries with a view to the union of the Lutheran and Calvinist sects, but his mission proving a failure, he took service in the troops of Maria Theresa, where he attained the rank of major under the name of l'Epine Babeuf, and that he was subsequently appointed tutor to the children of Maria Theresa. It is further related that in after years the Emperor Joseph II., as he happened to be passing through Picardy, became acquainted with the son of his former major, the hero of this book, to whom he made the most brilliant offers of employment at the Court of Vienna. François Noel's severe democratic principles, even at that date, induced him resolutely to decline them. These details are taken from some manuscript notes respecting his youth, written by Babeuf at the close of his life. Considering the enthusiasm of the philosophic Emperor Joseph II. for the very same revolutionary ideas to which Babeuf himself was devoted, and his expressed intention, as related in these same memorial notes, of using his power to carry these ideas into effect, the rigid refusal of Babeuf to accept employment under him seems strange, and, taking all the circumstances into consideration, not a little improbable, more especially when we consider the immaturity of Babeuf's revolutionary principles at that time. One is inclined to suspect some exaggeration or distortion of the facts, probably unintentional, in Babeuf's account of his relations with Joseph II.

Babeuf speaks of his father, Claude Babeuf, as of a man "as proud as a Castilian, always counting himself rich and happy even in the midst of profound misery." He never, he says, "went to a wine shop, but delighted on rare occasions to don his soldier's uniform, which he carefully preserved, together with his formidable sabre, which he handled with the greatest ease and dexterity." He taught his son the elements of Latin, mathematics, and of the German language.

When about fifteen years of age, François Noel entered the service, as junior clerk, of a land commissioner, who taught him land surveying. Two years later it is stated that he became attached to a landowner, near the small town of Roye in Picardy. The elder Babeuf appears to have died some time in 1781, and henceforth his mother and sisters became the charge of François Noel. He kept them for over sixteen years. Old Claude Babeuf, we are told, on his deathbed, handed

4

to his son, as a last gift, a well-worn copy of
Plutarch's *Lives*, telling him that the book had
been his solace throughout the joys and sorrows
of his life.   He continued to press upon his son
to study the lives of the great men of antiquity.
" As for me," he went on to say, " I could have
wished to have resembled Caius Gracchus, even
though I were doomed to perish like him and his
for the greatest of all causes, the cause of the
common welfare ; but circumstances have not been
favourable to the accomplishment of my designs."
Expressing his conviction that his son would
follow in his steps : " Swear," said he, " upon this
sword, that has never yet departed from the path
of honour, never to abandon the interests of the
people, which are everything, and to pour out, if
need be, the last drop of your blood to enlighten
and defend this downtrodden race." The oath
on the sword was taken as desired.

On the 13th of November 1782, young Babeuf
married one of the lady's maids of the Countess
in whose husband's service he was.   His wife was
a native of Amiens, of poor parents, and seems to
have been, to a great extent at least, illiterate.
Babeuf afterwards called her " a woman of nature."
Soon afterwards Babeuf found a position at Noyon
in connection with land administration.   The
following year, after the birth of his first child, he
again removed to the town of Roye, where he soon

obtained a similar position as land-commissioner,[1] the highest he had yet held, which was confirmed to him by letters patent.

At the age of twenty-five, François Noel Babeuf thus found himself in a position, not only fairly remunerative, but involving a certain social standing. He was by this time a prosperous father of a family, the head of an office, with clerks employed under him, and with leisure enough to devote himself to literary pursuits and public affairs. During these years Babeuf had relations with the *Académie Royale des belles lettres* at Arras. The Academy of Arras was one of the numerous literary societies that sprang up in the course of the eighteenth century in most French towns of any importance, one of the functions of which was to start competitions for the solution of given questions. As is well known, Rousseau's first important essay in literary composition was the attempted solution of a problem put forward for competition by a similar society at an earlier date.

In 1785 the Arras Academy started the following question :—" Is it advantageous to reduce the number of roads in the territories of the villages of

---

[1] There seems to be some difficulty in ascertaining the status of Babeuf, or the precise nature of the office he held in the French bureaucratic system of the *ancien régime*. The exact title of Babeuf's office was " Commissaire à Terrier," the "Terrier" being a kind of " Domesday " of the various feudal holdings within the jurisdiction of the French monarchy.

the province of Artois, and to give to those preserved
a breadth sufficient to enable them to be planted
with trees ?   Indicate, in the case of the affirmative,
the means of effectuating such reduction." Babeuf
was one of the first to enter the lists as candidate,
and sent in his paper on the 25th November 1785.
In spite of his practical knowledge of matters
connected with the subject in question, the paper
was among those rejected by the society. The
incident, however, was the occasion of a friendship and correspondence, which lasted some years,
with Dubois de Fosseux, the secretary of the
society, who, twenty years older than Babeuf,
came, in course of time, to seek his opinion on all
subjects.

Fosseux seemed to have been immediately
struck with Babeuf's capacity, and wrote him a
friendly letter, suggesting he should continue his
efforts to obtain recognition by the society. He,
however, would not appear to have been a person
remarkable for tact—and proceeded, in the ensuing
letters, to inflict upon Babeuf posers entirely out
of the range of his line of thought, such as,
" Why are negroes born black ? "   " Which is
the more happy in the social order, the sensitive
man or the apathetic man ? " and so forth. At
the same time he loaded Babeuf with effusions of
his own, poetical and otherwise. Notwithstanding
the correspondents indulged in mutual flattery,

they were not always in accord. Fosseux found
some verses, sent to him by Babeuf, not fit to be
read before ladies "with delicate nerves." To
this the future Tribune of the people suggests
that they might be furtively brought under the
notice "of robust men, who might acquire fresh
force from them."

In March 1787 Babeuf makes an appeal to
Fosseux to circulate a *brochure* entitled *La Constitution du Corps-militaire en France, dans ses
rapports avec celle du Gouvernement et avec le
caractère National*, of which he sends him a copy.
He says that it is written by a person of his
acquaintance, who was particularly anxious that
it should be widely read in the town of Arras.
The work was of a distinctly revolutionary character, criticising severely the aristocratic caste-
system of grades in the French army, by which
all the higher positions were in the hands of
courtiers and aristocrats; and also advocates the
convocation of an assembly of the people, to
which the king should be responsible for his acts,
and which should be the ultimate court of appeal.
M. Advielle would attribute this little work to
Babeuf himself; but, although this may be so, no
conclusive evidence as to authorship is adducible.
Fosseux acknowledges the receipt of the book, with
compliments to the anonymous author, in his usual
effusive style; but a little later he writes "that it

has been impossible for him to find anyone to undertake its distribution." "All our booksellers," he says, "fear to compromise themselves with the police, and, in my capacity as sheriff, it would be equally unsuitable for me to become the distributor, since, from beginning to end, it does not cease to attack the government. For the rest, the work seems to me to be well put together, excellently written, and very interesting. I should be extremely flattered to make the acquaintance of the author, who is assuredly a man of much spirit and merit. In these circumstances, Monsieur, and not having better fulfilled my commission, I feel bound to return to you the copy you confided to me. I have been well recompensed for the little trouble I have taken by the pleasure I have had in reading it."

It is curious that in the very same letter in which he shirks the danger of helping to circulate *La Constitution du Corps-militaire*, Fosseux is enthusiastic over the project of a book bearing the title *Le Changement du monde entier*. It was to be divided into six parts : the first to contain a detailed table of the misery afflicting the society of the day, "of the abuses, the disorders, the calamities, the wrongs, the injustices, the bankruptcies, the subjects of despair, the brigandages, the thefts, the assassinations, the crimes and horrors of all sorts, which take place" ; the second was to contain the cause of these evils ; the third, to expound principles and preliminary notions ; the fourth, the expedients, means, and regulations by which " all citizens who are in necessity, or who only enjoy a modest fortune, may, together with their wives and children, be in the future well nourished, clothed, lighted, and warmed, receive a perfect education, and enjoy, by means of their honest labour, each according to his or her strength, abilities, sex, age, talent, trade, or profession, much more ease, liberty, justice, comfort, and advantage than nowadays." The fifth section should deal with the means of procuring at once an adequate sum of money without the imposition of taxes on the peoples! The sixth should consist of a reply to all objections.

This syllabus, sketched out by Dubois de Fosseux, is not only noteworthy as showing the beginnings of Utopian Socialism, which had been already formulated in Morelly's *Le Code de la nature*, published in 1755, though at first attributed to Diderot. But what is especially interesting is the fact, that the Utopian scheme which so fascinated his friend Fosseux, in spite of its suggestion of the programme of the *Equals* of eight years later, does not seem to have attracted the future " people's tribune " at all at this time. Writing a little later, he treats the supposititious author of the scheme, who may well have been Fosseux himself, as " a mere dreamer."

Early in May of this year Babeuf went to Paris,

on a visit of a few days, where he made the acquaintance of a rich merchant named Audiffret, who proved a true friend to him, and to whose purse he had recourse when, later on, he found himself abandoned by everyone. At this time he started a work on the simplification of the land register, but it did not appear until three years later, when it was associated with the name of his friend Audiffret, who had doubtless contributed to defray the cost of publication. Writing to a proposal of one Lemoignan to reform the magistracy, about this time, Babeuf expresses himself as partisan of a unified code of law, which would once for all sweep away the chaos of mediæval customs and regulations, valid in one province and invalid in the next, and would "procure for all individuals indiscriminately, as regards the blessings and advantages enjoyed in this lower world, an absolutely equal position."

We may regard this and other expressions of opinion in the correspondence of Babeuf at this time as showing that the beginnings of the future People's Tribune, and leader of the "Equals" of 1796, were already present in the land-commissioner of 1787. The last letter in the correspondence between Fosseux and Babeuf was by the former, dated the 11th March 1788, and complains of the neglect of Babeuf to return certain literary pieces sent, and concludes with an urgent wish that this should be done promptly, even though without accompanying letter. From whatever reason, all relations between the two correspondents seem to have abruptly terminated at this time. Up to the present the future Tribune had not shown any marked signs of revolutionary sentiment or conviction, beyond a few expressions of opinion such as those above quoted—at least, unless we are to consider the *Constitution militaire* as coming from his pen.

Babeuf, we gather, read but few papers, and these irregularly, amongst which are mentioned *Le Mercure de France* and the *Journal de la langue française.* Neither, as far as we can see, was his other reading of a revolutionary character. Coming into contact, however, in the course of his professional duties, it may be mentioned, with the king's Field-Marshal, the Comte de Castéjà, who seems to have treated him with the haughtiness of the aristocrat of the *ancien régime*, Babeuf had a passage of arms with him, in which he defended himself with tact and dignity.

The year before the outbreak of the Revolution found Babeuf at the zenith of his prosperity as a land-agent, with a considerable *clientèle* among the nobility and clergy, all of them eager to avail themselves of his knowledge of land tenure and of his practical ability as a business man. About this time he was charged by the Prior of St

Taurin, a religious foundation in the neighbourhood
of the town of Roye, to form an abstract of all
the titles of the priory, together with all possible
rights and privileges that could be invoked. The
work occupied him six months. Shortly after, he
also undertook important researches into the
territorial archives of the Marquis de Soyecourt,
one of the many nobles of the *ancien régime* who
had exhausted his available substance in hanging
round the court at Versailles, and who, in spite of
his immense landed possessions, had at that time the
not unusual aristocratic notoriety of not paying anyone, not even the innkeepers to whose houses he
had resort on his travels. As might be expected,
on the termination of his arduous labours, Babeuf
found his bill of 12,000 livres (francs) disputed by
his patron, who refused to hand over more than
a hundred louis, a sum with which the creditor,
hard driven as he was, and quite unable to risk the
expenses of a lawsuit, had to be content. The
affair absolutely ruined Babeuf, as it had occupied
all his time for months, and had in consequence
caused him to refuse several advantageous offers of
other work. In this matter a certain influential
family of the town of Roye, named Billecocq, had,
it appears, been involved. The Billecocqs seem to
have had an implacable hostility to Babeuf, whom
they suspected of having done them an evil turn,
they having lost their position as attorneys to the

Marquis de Soyecourt, as they imagined, owing to the influence of Babeuf.

It was now the eve of the opening of the world-renowned series of events constituting the French Revolution; and our hero, under the combined influence of personal troubles, and of the social and political atmosphere in which he lived and moved, was rapidly becoming a changed man. Babeuf, at the time, it should be said, was the father of an increasing family.

CHAPTER II

THE REVOLUTIONARY DRAMA OPENS

FRANÇOIS NOEL BABEUF was still at Roye on the convocation of the States-General in May 1789. He had indeed been active at the *Cahier* of the district of Roye.[1]

The first article from the pen of Babeuf, which proposed the abolition of feudal tenures, and the substitution of a single tax, irrespective of class, for the mass of existing imposts, local and national, was sufficient to extinguish his career as Commissaire à Terrier. One of the Billecocqs, however, president of the committee for the reduction of the Cahiers, protested, with the result that Babeuf's motion was rejected.

The first open revolutionary act of our hero appears to have been the part he took in procuring

---

[1] It is perhaps scarcely necessary to remind the reader that the *Cahier* was the statement of grievances, and the remedies demanded, which was drawn up by every township and bailiwick throughout the territories of the French monarchy, by royal command, for the consideration of the States-General when they should assemble.

the destruction of the seigniorial archives of the neighbouring territories, which were publicly burned on the market-place at Roye: the details, however, of this transaction are wanting.

In July 1789 Babeuf made a hurried visit to Paris, just in time to be present at the taking of the Bastille. The following day he returned to Roye, and on his way succeeded in delivering a noble, the Comte de Lauraguais, who was besieged in his castle by his tenants, after the manner of the time. Babeuf succeeded in persuading the peasants to disperse. Among his papers was found a note claiming the Comte as a good patron and a friend of the people. In a few days he returned to Paris, presumably after having made his family arrangements, remaining in the capital until October. This residence in Paris finally converted the land-agent into a thoroughgoing partisan of revolutionary principles. Meanwhile the letters to his wife dealing with the events consequent on the fall of the Bastille are interesting. After describing the parading of the head of Foulon on a pike in procession along the Faubourg St Martin, in the midst of a hundred thousand spectators, who greeted it with shouts of joy, he continues: " How ill that joy made me! I was at the same time alike satisfied and ill content. I said, so much the better and so much the worse! I understand that the people should do justice for itself; I approve of that justice so long as the destruction of the guilty suffices for it, but has it not to-day become cruel? Punishments of all kinds—quartering, torture, the wheel, the stake, the whip, the gibbet, executions everywhere —have demoralised us! Our masters, instead of policing us, have made us barbarians, because they are such themselves. They reap, and will continue to reap, what they have sown. For all this, O my poor wife! will have, as far as one can see, terrible consequences! We are as yet only at the beginning!" A truly significant forecast this.

The main object of Babeuf's visit to Paris was, however, not political, but was for the purpose of getting further work in connection with land-agency. Babeuf was not long in coming to the conclusion that the days of his métier, in the old sense at least, were numbered. He heard everywhere indications that the time of feudal châteaux, of seigniorial rights and ecclesiastical privileges, was at an end; but he adds, " I am myself disposed, all the same, to put my shoulder to the wheel, to bring about that which would destroy my livelihood. Egoists would call me mad, but no matter!"

A further letter of the 16th August shows the state of impecuniosity in which his family were left. He also speaks of his working with M. Audiffret upon the land register before referred to. He further alludes to his hope of getting some employment in Paris. At this time he published a small pamphlet entitled, *La nouvelle distinction des ordres par M. de Mirabeau.* For Mirabeau, Babeuf appears to have had as great a dislike and distrust as that other tribune of the people, Jean Paul Marat.

Meanwhile, Babeuf's wife seems to have written him heartrending letters on the state of the family economically at Roye; and we find that he has to ask assistance, in the shape of money borrowed from his friend M. Audiffret.

Apart from the work in land registration before mentioned, Babeuf was already considerably occupied with Audiffret in connection with what is described as a new mathematical instrument called the Graphomètre-Trigonométrique, to which was added, a little later, another instrument called the Cyclomètre, designed to supplement the functioning of the former. The precise nature of these instruments it is impossible now to determine, though it appears they were intended to be used in land surveying. But, in any case, nothing seems to have come of the invention in the shape of profit to the inventors, and its subsequent fate rests in obscurity. At last the *Cadastre perpétuel,* which Babeuf had begun some years before, and which was a kind of " cast-off " of the territorial division and conditions of land tenure throughout France, was completed. Babeuf's son, Émile Babeuf, claims that this work " fixed the mode for the division of the departments, but brought nothing to its author," referring, of course, to the cutting up of the old French provinces into departments by the Constituent Assembly.

It may be mentioned that about this time François Noel took the additional name of Camille, for what reason it does not appear. His family still remained at Roye, and seem to have been left very much to themselves.

The year 1790 was an active one for Babeuf. We find him in April at Noyon, in May at St Quentin, and in July in Paris at the great fête of the Confederation. He was very diligent in his adopted town of Roye during this year, drawing up petitions to the Assembly, and redacting the proclamations of the municipal council. He appears to have come into collision, notwithstanding, with the municipality respecting a pamphlet claiming taxation according to means, which he was accused of having had printed and circulated by the official machinery of the municipality without its authorisation.

He also agitated among the *cabaretiers* (wine-shop keepers), urging them to resist their taxation, and had in consequence a decree of arrest launched against him, which, however, was not acted upon. His local popularity was now becoming great, but, on the other hand, he had to encounter the hostility of his old enemies, the

Billecocq family, who succeeded in making any continuance of his old profession impossible in the district. He now definitely abandoned his old means of livelihood, and started upon a career of political journalism, founding, with a friend who was a printer at Noyon, a journal, having for its title *Le Correspondant Picard*. Forty numbers in all appeared, and, according to a statement of his, brought him two hundred lawsuits in six months! A certain strict patriot took Babeuf severely to task for calling his journal *Le Correspondant Picard*, objecting that there was no longer a Picardy, the new *régime* only recognising the departments of the Somme, Oise, and Aisne. The paper, it is needless to say, was nevertheless thoroughly revolutionary, and was not wanting in the profusion of classical allusions and references to Roman history so characteristic of the time.

Probably in the above-mentioned lawsuits was included a criminal prosecution for one of his articles in connection with which we find him in prison at the beginning of July 1790. He was released, however, in time to take part in the festival of the Federation, the anniversary of the taking of the Bastille, the 14th of July, owing to the pressure brought to bear on the authorities by Marat. In an article in the *Ami du Peuple* of July 4th, Marat claims the release of the "Sieur Babeuf," then lying in gaol for a press offence.

5

Accused by an aristocrat of being a turncoat, of having become the most vehement enemy of every remnant of the feudal system after having gained his living as a feudalist and a seigniorial agent, Babeuf replied, that in his youth he did not reason ; since then he had believed that all that was ought to be—that it was absolutely necessary that there should be persecutors and persecuted ; until recently, therefore, he stood in awe of his "mother, the feudal system," but since he had become a man, since "the sun of the Revolution" had enlightened him, he perceived that this mother was a "hydra with a hundred heads."

Neither his journal nor any other occupation that he then had proved sufficient to keep Babeuf and his family in the necessaries of life. Hence, in September 1792, he was glad to accept the post offered him of administrator and archivist of the department of the Somme, and he finally left Roye. His position brought him to Amiens, where he settled down for the time being, but where he found a formidable rival from Roye, a representative of the people, a certain Andrè Dumonge. The rivalry developed into a quarrel between the two men, in which Babeuf got the worst of it and had to leave. He succeeded, notwithstanding, in obtaining a similar if somewhat inferior post in the district of Montdidier. Here, however, he was still more unfortunate than at Amiens. The president of the district was an extreme royalist and aristocrat, whom, it was said, though the details are wanting, Babeuf saved on one occasion from the fury of the populace. Whether this be true or not, the man seems to have nourished a personal grudge against Babeuf, either from political or private reasons, and to have only waited for an opportunity of serving him a bad turn. Babeuf found himself accused one day of having substituted one name for another in an act of sale of one of the national lands; for his position involved a great amount of work in connection with the repartition and sale of the nationalised property of the Church. Babeuf immediately repaired to Amiens to justify himself for what was undoubtedly due to an accidental negligence, but there he was at once arrested on the charge of forgery in connection with the affair. Probably aware that he was not likely to have a fair trial, Babeuf profited by an opportunity which offered itself for escape from his gaolers. The trial continued all the same, and many months later, on the 23rd of August 1793, Babeuf was condemned, *in contumaciam*, to twenty years' penal servitude.

He had, however, fled to Paris, whence he writes, under date 24th February 1794, relating the steps he was taking with the minister concerned, with a view to saving his honour. He justly ridicules the absurdity of the accusation of his having made money by forgery, calling to witness the indigence of himself and his family. He states that an American named Fournier is giving him a little literary work; that he is also undertaking the presentation of a petition for the said Fournier.

Meanwhile, Babeuf's family, that he had left at Montdidier, were indeed in terrible straits, everywhere in debt, with clamorous creditors on all sides. On the 6th of March we find Mme. Babeuf compelled to compound for her liabilities by abandoning the whole of her furniture.

Just at this time, however, Babeuf again succeeded in obtaining an appointment, on this occasion in connection with the Commune of Paris, as secretary to the Administration of Subsistence. His wife and family now came to join him in Paris. At the Bureau des Subsistances, on which he was engaged, Babeuf discovered a great deal of peculation, or at least a great deal of leakage in the accounts. This may well have been the work of subordinates, and unknown to the authorities. Babeuf, however, got it into his head that it was the result of a conspiracy on the part of those in high places to produce an artificial famine. He thereupon denounced certain prominent persons to the Paris sections, and the latter ordered the publication of the reports of Babeuf, and an investigation into the charges through a commission, which was, however, suppressed by the government (*i.e.* the

Committee of Public Safety).   The many influential enemies he had raised up in Paris in connection with this affair were probably responsible for the speedy success of the Montdidier authorities in obtaining his arrest, with a view to his being delivered over to them as a prisoner.

Babeuf, his wife and family, now lived at 27 Porte St Honoré.   It was here that he was arrested, and, together with the clerks of the Bureau des Subsistances, imprisoned in the Abbaye.   Babeuf himself was some weeks later sent to take his trial before the criminal tribunal of the Aisne on the old charge of forgery, but on a fresh indictment. On the 28th Floréal (18th of July 1794), however, the judges of the supreme tribunal of the Aisne, at Laon, on examination of the evidence, unanimously declared that there was no case on which to proceed against the accused.   Thus Babeuf's honour was finally rehabilitated.   The whole business would seem to have been originally plotted by various political and personal enemies of Babeuf in Picardy.   Several royalist members of the Roye municipal council appear to have been implicated. Add to this, that the friends of various emigrant aristocrats from the district of Montdidier, whose domains were therefore forfeited to the nation, were naturally anxious to throw every obstacle they could in the way of their partition and sale, while the commissioner Babeuf was not less zealous in his determination to bring to naught their aristocratic intrigues to rob the nation of its newly acquired property.

After his acquittal, Babeuf returned to Paris at the time that Robespierre was still remaining in power. Here, however, he seems to have been content to "lie low" politically, thereby escaping the unpleasant attentions of Robespierre and his committee. A short time later we find him back at Laon, where his son Émile was lying dangerously ill. He was at Laon when the news of the Revolution of the 9th Thermidor, ann. II. (27th of July 1794), and the fall of Robespierre, reached him. Babeuf, on finding the turn things had taken, returned immediately to Paris, where he started his *Journal de la liberté de la presse*, in which he vehemently attacked the fallen government, and the system of the Terror generally, in the interests of the Thermidoreans, though it was not long before he began to attack the latter as vehemently as the former. In this way, as we shall see, Babeuf stirred up fresh enemies against himself, and before long landed himself once more in gaol.

CHAPTER III

VICISSITUDES OF FORTUNE AND RIPENING
OF IDEAS

As already stated, shortly after the fall of Robespierre, Babeuf reappeared in Paris and founded the *Journal de la liberté de la presse*, in which he played the part of political free lance, attacking in turn the Robespierrists and the Thermidoreans. At first, however, the whole of his energies seem to have been directed against the party of Robespierre and the old revolutionary government. He was indeed at this time on terms of intimacy with several of the Thermidorean leaders, notably Tallien and Fouché, who subsequently became his bitter enemies. Before long, however, his general journalistic attitude caused the absurd suspicion to fall upon him of being a royalist agent in disguise. This was enhanced by his public speaking, at which he now became very assiduous, more particularly in the club of his quarter, where he nightly attacked the authority of the Convention, and especially the leading Thermidoreans. In this

way Babeuf made himself the enemy alike of the
Jacobins and of the parties now dominant in the
Convention.   The former were incensed by a
pamphlet issued by him at this time, *Du système
de dépopulation ou la vie et les crimes de Carrier*,
in which the methods of Carrier, his noyades,
republican marriages, etc., were denounced in the
most violent language.

The journal itself was consecrated to the cause
implied by· its name, and, as already stated, although first directed mainly against the "tail of
Robespierre," as the partisans of the fallen dictator
were now termed, soon took to criticising with
equal severity the successful faction in the recent
struggle.   The tenth number merits notice, inasmuch as Babeuf reproduced therein the address of
the popular society of Arras to the National
Convention, containing a kind of manifesto on the
liberty of the press, coupled with a denunciation
of Barère, the notorious ex-member of the Committee of Public Safety.   As is well known, it was
drawn up by Babeuf himself.   It concluded with the
words: "Men of the 9th of Thermidor, we declare before you, on behalf of our fellow-citizens, that they,
deadened by a long lethargy, demand their freedom,
claiming that the fall of tyrants shall render to
us our eternal rights, that liberty shall step forth
in the full glory of its power from the tomb of the
dictator.   Representatives, the men of the north,

who have muzzled that devouring ogre, whose furies have desolated our country during five months, will prove themselves raised to your level, in denouncing to you the revolutionary phantom behind which Joseph Lebon has sheltered himself, in order to battle victoriously against the victims who struggle to escape his fury. We denounce to you Barère, that vile slave of Robespierre." The document proceeds to stigmatise, in a few phrases, the horrors of "the Terror" as exercised at Arras.

The above, in the oratorical manner of the time, is a good specimen of Babeuf's writing, in what we may term the "grand" style of manifesto. The journal from the first excited the adverse attention of the authorities, and it had been published little more than two months before the violence of its language caused action to be taken by the "Committee of General Security," and on the 13th of October 1794 an attempt was made to stop the paper and seize the person of Babeuf. Warned in time, however, he succeeded in hiding himself, and what is more, from a secret retreat, in publishing his paper under a new title. It now appeared as the *Tribun du Peuple*. Otherwise it remained unchanged, either in shape or character, being avowedly the continuation of the original enterprise.

It is to be remarked that a notable change began about this time to take place in the opinions of Babeuf in regard to the·old revolutionary leaders and their policy. He no longer attacked them indiscriminately. We give Babeuf's opinion of Robespierre at this turning-point of his career. " This Robespierre," he says, " whose memory to-day is unjustly abhorred, this Robespierre is one in whom we must distinguish two persons—Robespierre the sincere patriot, a friend of just principles down to 1793, and Robespierre the ambitious tyrant, and the worst of criminals since that epoch. This Robespierre, I say, so long as he was a citizen, is perhaps the best source in which to seek great truths and powerful arguments for the rights of the press." He goes on to point out that the declaration of the Rights of Man the nation really owes to Robespierre. " We cannot fail to esteem the work," he continues, " though we forget the workman," or rather, as he had already said, " let us distinguish between Robespierre the apostle of liberty, and Robespierre the most infamous of tyrants ! "

During this time the paper seems to have appeared mostly without the printer's name, though the deputy Guffroy was undoubtedly the printer of several numbers. Number 33 never appeared, the manuscript having been seized by the authorities. It contained a violent attack of the most convincing character on the Thermidorean reaction. All this time the police were unable to lay hands upon Babeuf himself, but, in revenge, they were zealous in arresting the distributors of the journal. Amongst these was one Anne Treillard, who played a leading part in the distribution. This woman was subjected to a close interrogation as to the whereabouts of Babeuf. She denied all knowledge of his domicile, and stated that he himself brought her the packages containing the numbers to a place in the Jardin de l'Égalité. Asked if she would know Babeuf if she saw him, she replied that she had never observed him closely, but that he was of medium stature, with a long, thin, serious-looking face. Asked, still further, where the first numbers were sold, she replied that they were fetched from somewhere near the Place des Piques, and that it was from thence that the *Journal de la liberté de la presse* had been sent out.

By an irony of fate, it was his recent friend Tallien who had now become the sworn enemy of the late revolutionary government and of Jacobin principles generally, and whom Babeuf had also attacked in his journal, who was the instrument of obtaining Babeuf's arrest. In a speech in the Convention on this occasion, Tallien denounced Babeuf as the tool of Fouché, whose enemy Tallien had now become. It was the 10th of Pluviose, year III. (29th January 1795), that Tallien brought forward his motion for Babeuf's arrest, on the

ground of his having outraged the national representation in his articles. The Convention giving
its consent, the arrest was effected by the executive
authorities a few days later.

Owing to the hints obtained from the woman
Anne Treillard, the committee, acting presumably
on the motion carried by Tallien before the Convention a fortnight before, succeeded by means
of its police in discovering and seizing Babeuf
on the 12th of February 1795. While in prison,
their victim, however, was successful in smuggling
out and getting distributed a manifesto entitled
" Babeuf, the Tribune of the People, to his Fellow-
Citizens." It consisted in a vigorous defence of
his public and private conduct, not forgetting the
affair at Montdidier. But it was without effect,
for, together with other members of his staff, a
few days later he was conveyed from Paris to
Arras, where the imprisonment was continued.
It should be noted, as regards this, that Babeuf and
his colleagues were imprisoned in a purely arbitrary
manner, as no definite charge had been formulated
against them, and no idea of a trial at any definite
time seems to have been even entertained, as it
certainly never took place.

Babeuf's companions in the prison at Arras
were Lebois, the editor of *Le Journal de l'égalité*;
Taffoureau, a friend of Babeuf's, probably from
the days of the *Correspondant Picard,* who had

been arrested as a partisan of the Terror in his native town of St Omer; and Cochet, also a native of St Omer, who was doubtless in gaol for the same reason. There were other partisans of the fallen party of the Mountain, who subsequently joined Babeuf's movement, and who were detained in another prison at Arras. Already, in 1787, in a letter to his old correspondent Dubois de Fosseux, Babeuf indicates that his mind was occupied with the question of the communisation of the land and the products of industry, but at that time it was in the form of a problem only. It was in the prison of Arras, singularly enough, the town where his old correspondent resided, that the root ideas of the communism subsequently embodied in the programme of the Equals of the year V. were first definitely formulated. The first impulse, or at all events the first definite notion of communism as the economic ideal of human society, seems to have been derived by Babeuf from a study of Morelly's work, *Le Code de la nature et le véritable esprit de ses lois de tout temps négligé ou inconnu.*

This work of Morelly, an obscure author of whom little is known, was written about 1755, and seems to have had a certain vogue for a time, probably in part owing to the fact that it was for long attributed to Diderot. The work of Morelly was undoubtedly, both intrinsically and in effect,

the most important of the precursors, not only of
Babouvism, but of the Utopian Socialism of the
early nineteenth century; its influence, either direct
or indirect, on Fourier and Cabet being specially
noticeable.   In accordance with eighteenth-century
anthropology, Morelly starts with the classical
notion of the "golden age," which he deduces from
the theory that the primitive instincts of all men
are good.   The present state of inequality and its
accompanying human misery is due, not to any
intrinsic defect in human nature, but to the institution of private property.   It was the inroads of
the latter upon the communism originally reigning
among the children of men that was the source
and fountain of all evil.   So soon as individuals
began to use more than their share of the common
goods, then began all the miseries that had afflicted
mankind.

Morelly accepted the principle of Helvetius,
that the root of all conduct was self-love, but
argued that, since no man can be happy by
himself alone without the aid of his fellow-men,
recognition of the claims of others—in other
words, moral rectitude—is the only certain means
of promoting one's own happiness.   As a direct
consequence of this principle, Morelly insisted
upon the common ownership of all wealth, and
the equal enjoyment of the good things of life
by all alike.   It is curious that this old eighteenth-

century writer seems to have been the first to
put forward the subsequently well-known maxim
" from each according to his abilities, to each according to his needs." He undoubtedly made this the
basis of his social construction. For his scheme
is plainly built throughout upon this principle.
The only advantage accruing to talent is, according
to Morelly's system, to be the honour of directing
the industry and the affairs of the community in
general. The natural products of different districts
are the paths from one to the other, by a natural
system of exchange, founded upon mutual accom-
modation.

Notwithstanding Morelly's conviction of the
intrinsic goodness of human nature, coercion is
assumed as necessary, to prevent the backsliding
of individual members of the new society. Strong
fortresses are spoken of in deserted places where
criminal or recalcitrant persons are to be confined
for a time, or, in extreme cases, for life. As regards marriage, Morelly insists that every citizen
who has attained to man's estate shall be compelled to marry. Celibacy is only to be allowed
after the fortieth year has been attained. At
the beginning of every year the festival of
marriage is to be celebrated for all those who
have attained the requisite age. " The young
persons of both sexes will be gathered together,
and, in presence of the senate of the city, every

youth will choose the maiden that pleases him, and as soon as he has received her consent, will take her to wife." The first marriage is to be indissoluble during ten years. Afterwards divorce is to be allowed, by consent of both, or even on the demand of one only, of the parties concerned. The divorced persons are not to be allowed to marry again before the expiration of one year, and they will not be permitted to be reunited to each other under any circumstances. They cannot marry younger persons than themselves, or than the divorced partner of the original marriage. Only widows and widowers are to have this liberty.

As might be expected, there are traces of the influence of the first, and, for a long time, sole exponent of Utopianism — Thomas More. As already stated, many of Fourier's specific doctrines are anticipated by Morelly, *e.g.* that the moral world is governed by civil laws, as the physical is by natural laws. In the physical world, argues Morelly, power of attraction, *i.e.* gravitation, is dominant; in the moral world, the place of gravitation is supplied by that of self-love. There is also a strong analogy between the "city" of Morelly and the phalanstère of Fourier. The division of the various elements of society on a fixed mechanical and arithmetical scheme, founded on a decimal basis, so characteristic of Fourier, is also noteworthy in Morelly. Even Fourier's description of the arrangement of his ideal phalanstère bears unmistakable traces of Morelly's work. According to the latter, in the centre of the city is to be a great open space, surrounded by storehouses and public buildings; surrounding these, again, are to be the dwellings of the citizens; farther away, the buildings in which industrial operations are carried on; still further away are the dwelling-places of the peasantry, together with the farm buildings. But these details, interesting as they are in view of the later developments of Utopian Socialism, have no special significance or importance for the movement inaugurated by Babeuf. The chief thing in this connection is the importance of the influence of Morelly's book in furnishing the groundwork for the definite communistic principles of the Society of the Equals. These ideas ripened in Babeuf's mind undoubtedly, and, through him, in those of his associates, during their imprisonment at Arras, early in the year 1795. Outside, the party of the Mountain and the Jacobins were throughout France at this time a defeated and a persecuted faction.

Communistic ideas, properly so called, though undoubtedly present in a loose and vague way in the minds of individual members of the old revolutionary party, were never formally recognised by the party as such, which always, in the main,

6

was a party of the small middle-class, and the small independent master-workman, who economically at this time formed part of that class. Hence it represented, as such, economically, the interests of the small property-holder as against the feudal landlord, and all that appertained to him, in the first place; and in the second place, as against the new wealthy manufacturer, contractor, and man of finance. But the proletariat, as we understand it to-day, was too young and immature to have, strictly speaking, a definite class-consciousness of its own, still less determinate principles of political action. Nevertheless, so far as it was possible, Babeuf's new movement constituted for the moment the rallying-point, as for a last effort, of all the revolutionary sections of the French people.

The formation of a new class of wealthy bourgeois to step into the place economically and politically of the displaced feudal aristocracy had already begun. It was already evident that the aim of the Thermidorean leaders, *i.e.* of those who had been instrumental in the overthrow of Robespierre and of the old revolutionary régime, was to place themselves at the head of such a new aristocracy of wealth. The process of the formation and consolidation of this new monied class was, as we all know, completed under the régime of the first Empire, but, as already said, it began unmistakably immediately after the overthrow of the

system of the Terror.   It dates, indeed, really from
long before, in fact from the end of 1789, when the
first sale of the nationalised ecclesiastical lands
took place.

Syndicates were formed to compete with private
individuals in the scramble for the landed property of the Church.   As only a small percentage
of the purchase-money had to be paid at once,
the way of the astute speculator was smoothed for
him.   In the not unfounded hopes of evading the
payment of the second instalment, many of these
adventurers favoured the Revolution, and were
specially eager in urging on the Austrian war.
After the overthrow of the monarchy on the 10th
of August 1792 it was decided that the lands of
the emigrant nobles should be sold only in small
lots, and not in huge sections, as had been the case
with the ecclesiastical lands.

Here we see the effects of the new revolutionary
régime, in which the influence of the small middle
and working class was dominant.   The speculators
and financiers were for the moment cowed.   But
this did not prevent these same speculators and
jobbers, during the ensuing winter, from evading
the law and making money, by means of sham sales
and other arts of trickery, out of the costly furniture
and movable effects of the fugitive nobles.   But
although arranged for on paper, the actual partition
of the lands themselves remained uneffected so

long as the "moderate" party of the Girondins
continued to be the official repositories of political
power. After their fall, the sale of the lands was
definitely ordered on the conditions already described. But the decree of the Convention was
again hampered in its execution owing to the
intervention of the second great campaign against
the coalition of Europe of the autumn of 1793.
France became for the nonce a "gigantic armed
camp," and the one thought was the national
defence. But though few transfers, in the sense intended, were made, this did not prevent individual
agents of the government from improving the
situation to their own advantage by sales which
evaded the conditions imposed. Two-thirds of the
houses in Paris had now become national property.

Finally, the Committee of Public Safety, early
in 1794, while ordering the sale of the confiscated lands to be continued with greater despatch
than heretofore, and while advising the principle
of partition on a small scale should be adhered to
as far as possible, did not make the latter an
absolute *sine qua non*, the result being that the
victuallers of the army and the contractors for war
material generally, who had become suddenly rich
by the malpractices usual with their tribe, had
succeeded in annexing considerable tracts of French
territory for nominal sums in cash. Other means
were now adopted for enabling the new privileged

classes to raise themselves economically at the expense of the *bas peuple*, foremost among which was the hocussing of the currency by the issuing of a limitless mass of a practically worthless paper.

These and other forms of robbery on the part of the new financial middle-class flourished still more exceedingly during the heyday of this class—the period of the Consulate and Empire. It was, then, this new middle-class which from the Revolution of Thermidor onwards gave intellectual, moral, and political tone to French life. The active opposition to their sway was constituted by the remains of the old revolutionary party, which were momentarily gathered together in the movement of which our François Noel, or Gracchus, Babeuf, as he now called himself, was the life and soul.

Babeuf himself alludes in his famous 43rd number of the *Tribun* to the object-lesson as to the turn things were taking, such as " he that runs could read," to be found in the comparison between the present and former fortunes of many of the old revolutionary leaders, now termed " Thermidoreans."

Barras had acquired five estates. Merlin de Thionville possessed two châteaux and immense landed property, and could afford to give 300,000 francs a month to his mistress. Tallien had made an alliance with a Spanish woman of wealth and title. Legendre, the *ci-devant* butcher, the former

friend of Danton, had come into possession of a
large estate, which he kept up at vast expense.
During the five revolutionary years before the 9th
of Thermidor the issue of paper money (*assignats*),
although disastrous enough in its economic effects,
was nevertheless kept within bounds, and, it has
been computed, amounted to not more than seven
milliards. A certain relative proportion between
the guarantee security and the paper money was
never quite lost sight of during all the issues dating
from before the fall of Robespierre. It was only
under the reaction which set in shortly after the
last event that all idea of proportion was cast to
the winds in favour of absolutely reckless swindling.
While, as above said, during the first five years of
the Revolution, it has been estimated that at most
seven milliards of paper was issued within two
years following July 1794, the amount of paper
poured into circulation has been reckoned to have
been not less than thirty-eight milliards; of which
thirty milliards belong to the first six months of
the Constitution of the year III., that is, to the
Government of the Directory.

It was indeed evident that all these "nouveaux
riches," thieves on a great scale, constituted the
real and sole effective power in the country. The
five directors were their mandatories.

The Directory and all the prominent politicians
of the time were hand in glove with a clique of

speculative financiers, whose sole aim was to enrich themselves. Their nefarious influence may be seen in most of the laws passed, and is indeed traceable right up to the year 1814. The bulk of the governing classes—under Barras, Bonaparte, the Bourbons —were dominated by, or were in league with, this band of robbers, who systematically exploited the national wealth for their own benefit. These financial jackals seized upon everything they could lay their hands on, it mattered not what—church revenues, fiscal monies, feudal estates. The result naturally was the sudden and rapid growth of a propertyless proletariat. Such was the state of things which confronted Babeuf when his political career began, and such was the population to whom the gospel of Babeuf appeared as a godsend. Thousands of persons in Paris and in other towns of France were on the brink of starvation. The economic situation in Paris under the Directory and the subsequent years was as desperate as any that has been known in the world's history.

Babeuf had and made many friends and sympathisers in Arras; amongst them was the family of the ex-proconsul there during the Terror, Joseph Lebon, who seem to have become enthusiastic adherents, which is significant, considering Lebon's association with the party of Robespierre, and Babeuf's severe attacks on the Robespierrists and even on Lebon personally, in the earlier

numbers of the *Tribun*.   This is more noteworthy,
seeing that Lebon was undoubtedly one of the
most ferocious agents of the Terror, and that
Babeuf, however much he may have modified his
view of the character of Robespierre in general,
had never as yet withdrawn his strictures of the
system of the Terror itself, which was entirely
opposed to the humanitarian principles he had
hitherto professed.   However this may be, his
acquaintance with the Lebons had an important
result for the movement, for it was in their house
Babeuf first met Darthé, his subsequent colleague
and right hand in the Society of the Pantheon, and
in the conspiracy of the Equals, which was its
sequel.

Augustin Alexandre Darthé was a native of
St Pol, in the department of the Pas-de-Calais.
Darthé had played a certain public rôle during
the Revolution, had taken part in the affair of the
Bastille, and had been afterwards a member of the
directing body of his department.   In consequence
of his services in this capacity he had been decreed
to have " merited well of the country."   He subsequently became public prosecutor to the revolutionary tribunals of Arras and Cambrai, where
his incorruptibility and frugality were recognised
by all.   He was a supporter of Robespierre, and
is described as of severe morals and of a com-
passionate heart !

During the time of Babeuf's detention at Arras the town was rent by the feud between the Thermidoreans, including the old aristocratic party, now reconciled to the wealthier middle-class in their abhorrence of the Terror, and the Sansculottes. The younger and more ardent members of the reactionary coalition, under the name of the *Jeunesse dorée*, had adopted an extravagant costume and long tresses. The partisans of the revolutionary régime were now indiscriminately termed Jacobins. At the Theatre disturbances took place between the two sides. One such disturbance, in which the son of the guillotined émigré, the Comte de Bethune, with some of his associates, took part, led to the arrest of the latter, and their detention as prisoners, in company with Babeuf and his friends. Babeuf describes the young aristocrat as a smooth-faced young man, with an attractive but deceptive manner. He continued the centre of the reactionary movement in Arras, where he held a kind of court, distributing the current paper money (*assignats*) lavishly amongst his fellows.

On the 24th of Fructidor, ann. IV. (16th September 1795), Babeuf, and his friend Charles Germain, with whom an intimacy had been established in the prison of Arras, and who was subsequently to become Babeuf's ardent and strenuous colleague in the conspiracy of the Equals, were transferred by the authorities to Paris, where shortly after they were released by an amnesty proclaimed by the National Convention at its closing sitting. It is now that the great period of Gracchus Babeuf's political activity, terminating only with his death, begins.

CHAPTER IV

THE SOCIETY OF THE PANTHEON

THE constitution of the year III., drawn up by the Abbé Siéyès, and adopted by the Convention, abolished universal suffrage, reimposed a high property qualification, and created two chambers, a lower house, called the Council of Five Hundred, and an upper house, called the Council of the Ancients, composed of two hundred and fifty members. It further provided that two-thirds of the representatives in the new Assembly should consist of members of the Convention itself. The executive government was to consist of a directory of five, nominated by the two chambers. This constitution was the final expression of the Thermidorean reaction. It is needless to say that the old democratic principles and revolutionary organisation, which had found their expression in the Constitution of 1793, were thus swept away by a stroke of the pen. The Constitution of 1793, which had never come into force, had now become the rallying-cry of the people's party. The last of the popular

insurrections, that of the 1st of Prairial, ann. III.
(May 20th, 1795), had as its cry the " Constitution
of '93 and the release of the patriots."

This insurrection, in spite of its momentary
success, was defeated the same day, and had as its
upshot the definite proscription of the old party of
the Mountain, who having, on the expulsion of the
other members of the Convention, accepted the
demands of the insurgents, were now treated as
rebels. As may well be imagined, Babeuf's indignation at the new constitution, which tricked
the people out of all the political rights which it
had won during the Revolution, knew no bounds.
In a letter written to the patriots of Arras, shortly
before his removal to Paris, he points out the effect
of the new constitution. " According to this
Constitution," he writes, " all those who have no
territorial property and all those who are unable
to write, that is to say, the greater part of the
French nation, will no longer have the right to
vote in public assemblies ; the rich and the clever
will alone be the nation. . . . According to this
Constitution you have two chambers, an upper
and a lower, a chamber of peers and a chamber
of commons ; it is no longer the people who sanction
the laws, it is the upper chamber that has the
veto ; they might as well have left it to the chamber
of Louis XVI."

As we have seen, Babeuf had many friends

and sympathisers in the departments, notably in his own department of the Pas-de-Calais, where his *Tribun* was much read. Many of these were now in Paris. With them, and with the considerable following he had already obtained among the Parisians, Babeuf started in October of this year (1795) a political society, having for its avowed aim the triumph of Economic no less than of Political Equality. A little later this society amalgamated with another similar body with revolutionary objects, and the two organisations, merged into one, now received the title of the Society of the Pantheon, from its meeting-place. It was not long before all that was revolutionary—Jacobin, as the phrase went—attached itself to the new movement. Of this movement Babeuf's *Tribun* became the official organ. On his release from prison, Babeuf had at once taken up the paper at the point, No. 34, where it was dropped eight months previously. We have already quoted passages in these later numbers, showing that the vigour of its denunciation of the dominant parties had lost nothing from the interval of its suspension. The new movement grew daily in strength during the following autumn and winter; nightly meetings were held, at which articles from the *Tribun* would be publicly read and discussed. The government began to get seriously alarmed. Neither the *Tribun* nor the Society of the Pantheon affected any longer to conceal the true aim of the movement.

A word should be said here as to the causes which led the new executive Directory to tolerate so long the public meetings of the Society of the Pantheon. It was founded, it should be premised, immediately after the defeat and the suppression by Napoleon of the royalist insurrection of October 1795 (13th Vendémiaire). On this occasion the government had armed a certain number of Jacobins, under the name of the "Patriots of '89," against their new royalist enemies, whose hopes of triumphs at the elections had been foiled by the decree of the Convention that two-thirds of the old Convention members were to be retained in the new legislative body. The royalists, who had recourse, in their turn, on this occasion, to an armed insurrection, had to be immediately defeated at all costs. The regular troops momentarily available being inadequate for that purpose (the insurgents under arms numbering something like 125,000), the aforesaid Jacobins were enrolled, and acquitted themselves manfully in dispersing the royalist insurgents. In consequence of these events, it occurred to the Directory, which had now come into being, that the temporary policy of conciliation towards the extreme parties was desirable. In the first place, they might require their services again in a similar way ; and in the

second place, they could be played off as a bogey
to the other parties, thereby strengthening the
hands of the government by showing it up in the
light of the only bulwark against anarchy and
Jacobinism.

The society, on its formation, first of all met in
the old refectory of the Convent of St Généviève,
of which the tenant of the now secularised religious
house, himself a Jacobin, granted the gratuitous
use. Later on, after it had increased in numbers,
the society's meetings were transferred to a large
subterranean vault in the same building, where,
according to Buonarroti, the flare of torches, the
hollow echo of voices, and the attitudes of the
audience standing, leaning against pillars, or lying
on the ground, produced a weird effect, well calcu-
lated to impress those present with the magnitude
and the dangers of their enterprise. From the
first the constitution of the society was very
irregular, no provision being made for the keeping
of books or minutes, and the only condition of
admission to its membership being the sponsorship
of two persons already members. This looseness
of organisation was largely due to a fear of coming
into conflict with the new law concerning the right
of public assembly, which imposed many restrictions, and especially to a desire not to give colour
to the notion that the Pantheon Society was a
revival of the Jacobin Club under another name,

which, it was felt, would at once arouse hostility in influential circles, and lead to suppression of the society and to the persecution of its members. On the other hand, the looseness of procedure was the fruitful cause of many undesirable persons being admitted, although the nature of the movement at the outset, not being a wholly secret society, but avowedly a political party (albeit with well-nigh undisguised insurrectionary aims), rendered anything like a strict scrutiny of candidates for admission a practical impossibility.

The society had not been long in existence before it counted over two thousand constant members. But it might have been remarked that it was not altogether homogeneous in respect of principles. There seems to have been a right and left wing, the first composed of miscellaneous Jacobins, calling themselves "Patriots of '89," many of whom had fought against the royalist insurgents on the 13th of Vendémiaire, and who, in consequence, had some influence with the government, and the more thoroughgoing and definite adherents of the doctrine of Equality, as understood by Babeuf and his friends. While the latter were untiring in agitating against the constitution recently come into force, and the fraudulent manner in which the small middle and working classes had been cheated of the fruits of the Revolution, the former were more concerned to get places for themselves and their associates. Nevertheless, for a time all worked fairly harmoniously together. A demand was made for the giving effect to a decree passed during the Terror, according to which one milliard of the proceeds derived from the sale of the national lands should be distributed among the " defenders of the country," to wit, those returned from the wars ; and in the case of those slain, for their families. The application of the poor law of ann. II. was also demanded. Other similar societies to that of the Pantheon now began to be formed, and to hold meetings in various parts of Paris.

Babeuf, as already intimated, boldly proclaimed in his paper, the *Tribun du Peuple*, the doctrine of equality, scathingly criticised the Directory, and continued unremittingly to denounce individual property-holding as the principal source of all the evil weighing on society. It was not long indeed before a new mandate of arrest was launched against him. Early in February 1796 the Directory decided to take vigorous measures for the suppression of the *Tribun*. Accordingly, an officer of the Court repaired to the Faubourg St Honoré No. 29 to execute the warrant. Babeuf, however, resisted, eventually succeeding in shaking the officer off, and dashed down the street, with the government representative at his heels shouting "stop thief!" Babeuf was successful, however, in getting away

to a shelter afforded him by Darthé and another
friend.   Foiled in their attempt to seize the person
of Babeuf, the authorities consoled themselves by
ordering the arrest of his wife and two children,
one of whom was ill at the time.   Members of the
Society of the Pantheon subscribed financial aid, as
did also his friends and followers at Arras.   The
prosecution, however, succeeded in its object; and
although Babeuf managed to issue a few more
numbers from his retreat, the journal came to an
end in a few days with the 43rd issue, which ex-
ceeds in boldness all that had gone before it.   The
Tribun du Peuple, after criticising the proclamation
of the Directory, its severe penal laws recently
enacted against the liberty of public meeting and
of the press, winds up: "All is finished.   The
Terror against the people is the order of the day.
It is no longer permitted to speak; it is no longer
permitted to read; it is no longer permitted to
think; it is no longer permitted to say that we
suffer; it is no longer permitted to repeat that we
live under the reign of the most abominable
tyrants."   The "abominable tyrants" were the
Thermidoreans, Barras, Merlin de Thionville, Tallien, Fréron, Legendre, etc., the would-be austere
republicans of yesterday, to-day for the most part
the wealthy parvenus, who had become possessed
of vast portions of the national property, confiscated
from the Nobility and the Church.

But even now Babeuf did not give up hope. "O people!" he exclaims, "do not despair; we shall break all the chains to prevent thee dying the victims of those who torture thee, who plunder thee, and who abuse thee these twenty months past." But the prophecy of Babeuf was not to be fulfilled. The Republic of the Rich, in which the new class that had entered into the spoils of the feudal and ecclesiastical aristocracy of old was to play the dominant rôle, was, before many years were over, destined to cast off even its republican form, and become an undisguised military despotism. Not for nothing had the young artillery officer won his spurs in the royalist insurrection of the 13th of Vendémiaire.

Hard upon the final collapse of the *Tribun du Peuple*, at its 43rd number, followed the publication of the celebrated "Manifesto of the Equals," which proved decisive for the fortunes of Babeuf and his friends. To this important document we shall revert again shortly. The following was the order of the meetings held by the Society of the Pantheon: the public reading of journals, the reading of correspondence, the collection for unfortunate "patriots," the discussion of steps to be taken to liberate those in prison, debate on questions of legislation and of general principles. Agents of the government worked their way into the confidence of the society, preaching non-resistance and submission to the Constitution of the year III. The policy of these government agents reached its climax in a motion proposing the sending of an obsequious address to the Directory, in which the society should formally declare its adhesion to the new constitution; and the influence of the section formed within the society by them was sufficiently powerful to overcome the stormy opposition with which the motion was received by that portion of the society which remained true to the principles on which it had been founded, and to get the motion of subservience carried. The tactics of the government in their dealings with the Pantheonists were distinctly clever, since it made evident an unmistakable cleavage in their body, which showed plainly who were those constituting the irreconcilable section and who were their leaders. The latter seemed to have regained their ascendancy in the society, as also in the branches scattered over Paris.

Among the many practical questions of the hour which occupied the attention of the Pantheonists, and were the subjects of the petitions of the partisans of the society to the legislative body, was the burning one—the fall in the value of the *assignat*. This was so violent that the price of the necessaries of life often doubled in the course of a single day, thus rendering it impossible for wages to keep on a level with them. Hence the handicraftsman, small trader, and the proletariat found ruin staring them in the face. Nevertheless, Babeuf and his friends deprecated any ill-considered and immature attacks upon the government, urging the discussion of the principles of the rights of man and of peoples rather than a too eager application of them to the tyrants of the hour, until public opinion should be sufficiently formed to admit of more drastic action. With the spread of their views in popularity, the leaders of the movement began to bethink themselves of means for extending still further their propaganda. Being many of them deists of the traditional eighteenth-century type, it was decided to present the political and economic doctrine of the Equals in a religious guise as part of the divinely ordained order of nature. They therefore decided, through the society, to apply to the authorities for permission to use one of the larger vacant churches in Paris for the purpose of celebrating a deistic festival.

It should be explained that the government itself, under the auspices of one of its members, Larivellière-Lépeaux, the "Theophilanthropist," at this time was introducing popular festivals once a decade in the churches in place of the Mass and the abolished services of the Catholic Church. The government, of course, at once saw through this demand and refused the application, on the pretext that the popular services mentioned, which

were about to be officially instituted, would meet
the needs of the situation.   But the project was
not given up; the subject was discussed during
many meetings of the society, and eventually the
friends of Babeuf got their way.   It was decided
that the society should occupy " the decades " (the
tenth days) in honouring in public the divinity by
the preaching of the " natural law."   A commission
was then appointed to hire a church and draw
up regulations for the new cult.   The project, it
should be said, met with considerable opposition in
the society, as being a return to forms of super-
stition, and it had to be explained to the members,
as plainly as possible, consistently with safety, that
the religious form was merely a disguise, hiding a
social and political object.

By this time the Directory had become thoroughly
alarmed at the progress of the discussions of the
Society of the Pantheon.   Henceforward the police
were instructed to spy upon every movement of
the orators.   All that was wanting now was a
colourable pretext for government action.   The
convent near the Pantheon where the society met
was now known, in respectable and moderate
circles, as the " Cave of Brigands."   By the beginning of February 1796 most of the doubtful
and reactionary elements of the movement would
seem to have left, and the influence of Babeuf
and his friends dominated the whole body.

There still remained, however, within the fold, a few police spies, whose function it was to report all that occurred at the meetings, and any private information they could obtain from individuals, to the authorities. The pretext sought for by the government was furnished by Darthé in the reading of a number of the *Tribun* of Babeuf, in which the Directors and the leading members of the legislative body were vigorously attacked. Darthé was applauded to the echo when he had finished, but a few days after, on the 29th February 1796, the closure of the meeting-place of the Pantheonists and the dissolution of the society was ordered by the Directory, and was carried out in person by General Bonaparte. He it was, indeed, as is alleged, who was the leading spirit in the affair, and who, by means of spy-information he had obtained as to the real aims of the society, succeeded in inspiring panic in the Directory. As stated, he came in person, and compelled the keys of the meeting-place to be given into his hands. The usual attempt was made to discredit the Babouvists, as we may now call them, in public opinion, by representing their leaders as disguised royalist agents, seeking by means of anarchistic exaggerations to discredit the Republic.

The closing of the Pantheon was succeeded by the suppression of popular societies and public meetings throughout the city.

Babeuf's paper, as we have seen, died at this time (the 5th Floréal, year IV.; 16th April 1796), in spite of a desperate attempt to carry it on in secret after his arrest.

At the same time that Babeuf was conducting the *Tribun du Peuple*, he seems to have written articles in another journal of revolutionary principles published by Duplay, and entitled *L'Éclaireur du Peuple*, which was conducted by his friend Sylvain Maréchal, but of which only a few numbers appeared.

CHAPTER V

THERE was now only one course left to the Babouvists, and that was the concentration of the movement in the hands of a secret committee of insurrection.

It should be mentioned that before this, while the Society of the Pantheon was still flourishing, a secret committee to prepare an insurrection against the new tyranny had been formed, and met at the house in the Rue Clery, of Amar, the former member of the Committee of General Security during the Terror. It consisted of Amar himself, Darthé, Buonarroti, Massart (an adjutant-general of the army), and Germain, and was subsequently enlarged by the addition of other members.

Among the above-mentioned persons, Philippe Buonarroti is worthy of special note. Descended from Michael Angelo Buonarroti, born in Pisa in 1764, exiled from Italy owing to his enthusiastic adoption of French revolutionary principles, he became a prominent Jacobin, and was honoured by the Convention with the title of French citizen, joined the Society of the Pantheon, and became an enthusiastic supporter of Babeuf at the period at which we have arrived.

The theory of this committee was that the existing government established by the Constitution of the year III. was illegitimate and an usurpation; that, in addition, its intentions were oppressive and tyrannical, and that the public welfare demanded its destruction. Amar and one or two other members whose ideas were not clear were soon brought over by Darthé and Buonarroti to be enthusiastic adherents of the communistic doctrines of Babeuf and the "Equals." This committee, however, for various reasons, chief of which was the unjust denunciation of Amar by a former colleague of his, named Héron, who seems to have borne him implacable hatred, was dissolved. An attempt during the next few weeks to form various similar groups also came to nothing, and it was not until April that the celebrated committee composed of Babeuf, Debon, Buonarroti, Darthé, Félix Lepelletier, and Sylvain Maréchal was founded, and became the centre of the renowned Conspiracy of the "Equals," which only just missed overthrowing the Constitution of the year III., and the government founded upon it.

A striking unanimity of view associated the members of this head centre of the conspiracy;

political liberty and economic equality were the objects animating all. Sylvain Maréchal, already known as a prominent orator at the Pantheon, drew up the celebrated " Manifesto of the Equals" as a condensed exposition of the aims of the movement, and proposed its acceptance by his colleagues. Sylvain Maréchal, it may be noted, was not unknown to literary fame, having suffered four months' imprisonment during the *ancien régime* for a publication entitled the *Almanack of Honest Men* (*Almanach des honnêtes gens*). He also wrote a work entitled the *Atheist's Dictionary* (*Dictionnaire des Athées*). The Secret Directory, as the committee was called, not altogether approving certain expressions in the manifesto, did not authorise its publication as an authoritative statement of the views held by it, but its historical importance, nevertheless, as the best known short statement of the aims of the movement, induces us to give it here in its entirety. The manifesto of the Equals bears for its motto a phrase of Condorcet's—" Equality of fact, the final aim of social art." It proceeds as follows :—

"People of France ! During fifteen centuries you have lived as slaves, and in consequence unhappily. It is scarcely six years that you have begun to breathe, in the expectation of independence, happiness, equality ! The first demand of nature, the first need of man, and the chief knot binding

together all legitimate association! People of
France! you have not been more favoured than
other nations who vegetate on this unfortunate
growth! Always and everywhere the poor
human race, delivered over to more or less adroit
cannibals, has served as a plaything for all ambi-
tions, as a pasture for all tyrannies. Always and
everywhere men have been lulled by fine words;
never and nowhere have they obtained the thing
with the word. From time immemorial it has been
repeated, with hypocrisy, that *men are equal*; and
from time immemorial the most degrading and
the most monstrous inequality ceaselessly weighs
on the human race. Since the dawn of civil society
this noblest appanage of man has been recognised
without contradiction, but has on no single
occasion been realised; equality has never been
anything but a beautiful and sterile fiction of the
law. To-day, when it is demanded with a stronger
voice, they reply to us: ' Be silent, wretches!
Equality of fact is nought but a chimera; be contented with conditional equality; you are all equal
before the law. Canaille, what do you want more?'
What do we want more? Legislators, governors,
rich proprietors, listen, in your turn! We are all
equal, are we not? This principle remains uncon-
tested. For, unless attacked by madness, no one
could seriously say that it was night when it was
day.

" Well! we demand henceforth to live and to die equal, as we have been born equal. We demand real equality or death ; that is what we want.

" And we shall have it, this real equality, it matters not at what price! Woe betide those who place themselves between us and it! Woe betide him who offers resistance to a vow thus pronounced!

" The French Revolution is but the precursor of another, and a greater and more solemn revolution, and which will be the last!

" The People has marched over the bodies of kings and priests who coalesced against it : it will be the same with the new tyrants, with the new political hypocrites, seated in the place of the old ones! What do we want more than equality of rights ? We want not only the equality transcribed in the declaration of the Rights of Man and the citizen ; we will have it in the midst of us, under the roof of our houses. We consent to everything for its sake ; to make a clear board, that we may hold to it alone. Perish, if it must be, all the arts, provided real equality be left us![1] Legislators and governors, who have neither genius nor good faith ; rich proprietors without bowels of compassion, you will try in vain to neutralise our holy enterprise by saying that it does no more than reproduce that agrarian law already demanded more than once

[1] This was one of the sentences objected to by other members of the committee.

before!   Calumniators! be silent in your turn, and, in the silence of confusion, listen to our demands, dictated by nature and based upon justice!

" The agrarian law, or the partition of lands, was the immediate aim of certain soldiers without principles, of certain peoples moved by their instinct rather than by reason.   We aim at something more sublime and more equitable—the common good, or the community of goods.   No more individual property in land ; the land belongs to no one.   We demand, we would have, the communal enjoyment of the fruits of the earth, fruits which are for everyone!

" We declare that we can no longer suffer, with the enormous majority of men, labour and sweat in the service and for the good pleasure of a small minority!   Enough and too long have less than a million of individuals disposed of that which belongs to more than twenty millions of their kind!

" Let this great scandal, that our grandchildren will hardly be willing to believe in, cease!

" Let disappear, once for all, the revolting distinction of rich and poor, of great and small, of masters and valets, of governors and governed![1]

" Let there be no other difference between human beings than those of age and sex.   Since all have

---

[1] The idea of the abolition of governors and governed was also, as we are informed by Buonarroti, objected to by some of his colleagues.

the same needs and the same faculties, let there be
one education for all, one food for all. We are
contented with one sun and one air for all. Why
should the same portion and the same quality of
nourishment not suffice for each of us ?   But
already the enemies of an order of things the most
natural that can be imagined, declaim against us.
Disorganisers and factious persons, say they, you
only seek massacre and plunder.   People of France !
we shall not waste our time in replying to them,
but we shall tell you: the holy enterprise which
we organise has no other aim than to put an end
to civil dissensions and to the public misery.

" Never has a vaster design been conceived or
put into execution.   From time to time some men
of genius, some sages, have spoken of it in a low and
trembling voice.   Not one of them has had the
courage to tell the whole truth.

" The moment for great measures has come.
The evil is at its height.   It covers the face of the
earth.   Chaos, under the name of politics, reigns
there throughout too many centuries.   Let everything return once more to order, and reassume its
just place !

" At the voice of equality, let the elements of
justice and well-being organise themselves.   The
moment has arrived for founding the Republic of
the Equals, that grand refuge open for all men.
The days of general restitution have come.   Families

groaning in misery, come and seat yourselves at the common table prepared by nature for all her children! People of France! the purest form of all glory has been reserved for thee! Yes, it is you who may first offer to the world this touching spectacle!

"Ancient customs, antiquated conventions, would anew raise an obstacle to the establishment of the Republic of the Equals. The organisation of real equality, the only kind that answers all needs without making victims, without costing sacrifices, will not perhaps please everybody at first. The egoist, the ambitious man, will tremble with rage. Those who possess unjustly will cry aloud against its injustice. Exclusive enjoyments, solitary pleasures, personal ease, will cause sharp regrets on the part of individuals who have fattened on the labour of others. The lovers of absolute power, the vile supporters of arbitrary authority, will scarcely bend their arrogant chiefs to the level of real equality. Their narrow view will penetrate with difficulty, it may be, the near future of common well-being. But what can a few thousand malcontents do against a mass of men, all of them happy, and surprised to have sought so long for a happiness which they had beneath their hand?

"The day after this veritable revolution they will say, with astonishment, What? the common well-being was to be had for so little? We had only

to will it.   Ah! why did we not will it sooner?
Why had we to be told about it so many times?
Yes, doubtless, with one man on earth richer, more
powerful than his neighbours, than his equals, the
equilibrium is broken, crime and misery are already
in the world.   People of France! by what sign
ought you henceforward to recognise the excellence
of a constitution?   That which rests entirely on an
equality of fact is the only one that can benefit
you and satisfy all your wants.

"The aristocratic charters of 1791 to 1795 have
only riveted your bonds instead of rending them.
That of 1793 was a great step indeed towards real
equality, and never before had it been approached
so closely; but yet, it did not achieve the aim
and did not touch the common well-being, of
which, nevertheless, it solemnly consecrated the
great principle.

"People of France! open your eyes and your
heart to the fulness of happiness. Recognise and
proclaim with us the 'Republic of the Equals'!"

As already stated, the Secret Directory did not
sanction the publication of the above document as
its own, exception being taken to certain expressions,
chiefly the phrase "Perish, if it must be, all the
arts, provided real equality be left us."   This we
learn from Buonarroti.   But the reason given
seems insufficient, since the elision or modification
of two or three phrases would have been an easy

8

matter, and indeed is a very common proceeding under similar circumstances ; and we may reasonably suspect some other reason as having influenced the committee against publishing the statement, which certainly in substance represented the views of all its members.   Be this as it may, the " Secret Directory" decided, in its place, to publish and circulate the somewhat shorter and certainly less rhetorical document, probably drawn up by Babeuf himself, and entitled " Analysis of the Doctrine of Babeuf, Tribune of the People, proscribed by the executive Directory for having told the truth " (*Analyse de la doctrine de Babeuf, tribun du peuple, proscrit par le directoire exécutif, pour avoir dit la vérité*).   It is divided into fifteen paragraphs, and is as follows :—

" 1. Nature has given to every man an equal right to the enjoyment of all goods.

" 2. The object of society is to defend its equality, often attacked by the strong and the wicked in the state of nature, and to augment, by the co-operation of all, the common means of enjoyment.

" 3. Nature has imposed upon each one the obligation to work.   No one can evade work without committing a crime.

" 4. Labour and enjoyment ought to be common to all.

" 5. There is oppression when one man, after exhausting himself with work, wants for everything, while another swims in abundance without doing anything.

" 6. No one, without committing a crime, can appropriate to himself exclusively the products of the earth and industry.

" 7. In a true society there ought to be neither rich nor poor.

" 8. The rich who are unwilling to renounce their superfluity in favour of the indigent are the enemies of the people.

" 9. No one should be able, by the accumulation of all the means necessary thereto, to deprive another of the instruction essential to his welfare; instruction ought to be in common.

" 10. The object of a revolution is to destroy any inequality, and to establish the well-being of all.

" 11. The Revolution is not finished, because the rich absorb all the good things of life and rule exclusively, while the poor labour as veritable slaves, languishing in misery, and counting as nothing in the State.

" 12. The Constitution of 1793 is the true law of the Frenchman because the people have solemnly accepted it; because the Convention had not the right to change it; because, in order to do so, it has had to shoot down the people who demanded its execution; because it has driven out and murdered the deputies who did their duty in defending the people; because the terror of the people and the influence of the emigrant aristocrats has presided at the drawing up and the pretended acceptance of the Constitution of Anno III. (1795), which has not obtained even the fourth part of the votes cast for that of 1793; because the Constitution of 1793 has consecrated the inalienable right of every citizen to consent to the laws, to exercise political rights, to hold public meetings, to demand that which he believes to be useful, to educate himself, and not to die of hunger,—rights which the counter-revolutionary Act of Anno III. (1795) has openly and completely violated.

" 13. Every citizen is bound to re-establish and to defend the Constitution of 1793—the will and the well-being of the people.

" 14. All the powers derived from the pretended Constitution of Anno III. (1795) are illegal and counter-revolutionary.

" 15. Those who have raised their hand against the Constitution of 1793 are guilty of treason against the people."

Such is the official statement of the general aims of the Insurrectionary Committee or Secret Directory, of which Babeuf was the leading spirit. The view expressed as to the illegality of the Constitution of the year III. (1795) is indisputable. The earlier Constitution of 1793, drawn up by the party of the Mountain in the Convention, which was of a thoroughly democratic character, had not only been accepted by the Convention itself, but had been ratified in a subsequent referendum by an overwhelming majority of the communes throughout France in their primary assemblies. Hence for the Convention, two years later, of its own authority, arbitrarily to tear up an Act of constitution, not merely adopted by itself, but solemnly ratified by a vote of the French people, was clearly a violation of all law, custom, or constitutional procedure whatever. It was, in short, an impudent and unscrupulous usurpation of power by the *nouveaux riches* of France and their satellites. As such, the " Secret Directory " was fully justified in declaring it to be an outrage on the people, and in no way binding on any Frenchman.

From this point of view, all authority deriving its sanction from the new Constitution of the year III. was null and void, and any exercise of power or act of violence on the part of such authority was, without doubt, justifiably to be regarded as mere brigandage. It was the primary objective, so to say, of the movement, the rehabilitation of the Constitution of 1793, that attracted all the old revolutionary elements to it, and united them in one accord. Old " Mountainists " and committee-men, partisans of Hébert and Chaumette, worked side by side with their old opponents, partisans of Robespierre, and both with the new Communist democrats, Babeuf and his friends. The realisation of the

Constitution of '93 was the link which bound them. In one respect, the " Secret Directory " was simply a continuation of the Society of the Pantheon, in so far as the work of propaganda and the educating and organising of public opinion was the chief object.   At the same time, while steadily keeping in view their ultimate aims, Babeuf and his friends, who formed the soul of the new movement, made it the chief point at this time to rally the scattered revolutionary forces under the banner of the Constitution of '93, an object upon which all could unite.

But it must not be supposed that the Babouvists regarded this work of the Convention in its revolutionary period as by any means perfect. For one thing, they naturally objected to its re-affirmation of the articles in the Declaration of the Rights of Man concerning the principles of private property - holding.   Even the constitution itself they considered as offering insufficient guarantees against usurpations on the part of the legislative body.   But they proposed to remedy these defects by additions and modifications after the constitution had been once in principle adopted.   It was enough for them that the Constitution of '93 was the best as a whole, and the most democratic up to date ; that it had been accepted almost unanimously by the French democracy, and that it was the one possible rallying-point for all the revolutionary parties.

Part of the work of the "Secret Directory" was to establish and keep going throughout Paris, now that public discussion on a large scale, as at the old convent of St Geneviève with the Pantheonists, was suppressed, small groups in private houses and elsewhere, beyond the observation of the authorities, which were often unknown to each other, but were under the direct supervision of the "Secret Directory" itself.   In order to carry on this organisation effectively the committee established twelve revolutionary agents, the selection of these agents occupying an important part of the time of the "Secret Directory." Several were chosen to disaffect the army, one being selected for each of the battalions stationed in Paris and the suburbs.   Thus a certain Fion was sent to the Invalides ; another, Vanek, had a roving commission among the various bodies of troops in the capital.

Charles Germain, of whom we have already spoken, and who made Babeuf's acquaintance in the prison of Arras, was allotted the task of winning over the legion of police ; and an army captain, George Grisel, of whom we shall hear more presently, was appointed to work on behalf of the "Secret Directory" at that important military centre, the camp at Grenelle, near Paris, where he himself was stationed.   Grisel had made the acquaintance of Darthé, who, with Germain, were now the right hands of Babeuf in the "Secret Directory" in the matter of organisation.   The Café of the " Bains aux Chinois " was at the time a rendezvous of the democratic party.   It was here that Grisel, a man of plausible speech, soon ingratiated himself with Darthé and the other leaders of the Equals, and became before long one of their most trusted and valued agents.

Great attention was now given also to the work of general propaganda by means of fly-sheets and placards, the analysis of the doctrine of Babeuf, already given, being distributed and placarded in great profusion.   Another broadsheet was entitled *An Opinion on our Two Constitutions*—a letter of *France Libre to his friend the Terror*.   Yet others were, *Do we owe Obedience to the Constitution of the year III.?* and the *Address of the Tribune to the Army*; the *Triumph of the French People against its Oppressors*, etc.   There was scarcely a day at this time which did not see some new publication of the Babouvists.   They were all eagerly read by thousands, for the distress consequent on the startling depreciation of the *assignats* was growing rapidly every day.   The success of the " Secret Directory " became now everywhere apparent.   The secret or semi-secret groups founded by the " Secret Directory " had borne such good fruit that public meetings in the streets and open spaces, in which the Constitution of '93 was demanded and the new communist doctrines discussed, sprang up, as it seemed, spontaneously.

It was now the beginning of May. Babeuf became more than ever the responsible leader of the whole insurrectionary movement. He it was who almost exclusively carried on the correspondence and issued the instructions to his agents, through the intermediary of a colleague and old friend, Didier, and in his retreat were deposited all the documents and the official seal of the conspiracy. It was clear that the time was becoming ripe for action. The only question was what form the action should take, and what form of governmental organisation should be established in the place of the hated Constitution of the year III., with its executive directory, which it was proposed to overthrow. To have called together the primary assemblies at once to elect a legislative body conformable to the Constitution of '93 being impracticable, it was obvious that an interval of time must elapse between the insurrection and the putting of the constitution into force. The question to be decided therefore was, what form should the interim public authority take? This question of the provisional government to be established on the success of the *coup de main*, which circumstances now pointed to as the next important step to be taken by the committee, became urgent.

Amar, the old member of the Committee of

General Security during the revolutionary period, proposed to reconstitute the National Convention as the only legitimate authority. But since, by arbitrary acts, a certain section of the Convention had rendered their authority null and void, and since a large number of the original members, to wit, those constituting the old party of the Mountain, had been driven out, exiled, or deprived of their political rights by the usurping dominant power, he proposed to recall all those members of the Convention who had been expelled and declared ineligible for re-election, together with that third of the old Convention at the time of its dissolution, which, not having formed part of the new legislative body (namely, the Council of " Five Hundred and the Ancients"), had not been responsible for the usurpation. To this it was objected that many of those it was proposed to readmit had been guilty of arbitrary acts in their capacity of Thermidoreans, such as the closing of the popular societies, the proscription of good democrats, the reintroduction into the Convention of the seventy-three expelled Girondins, and the liberation of aristocratic conspirators, etc.

These and other considerations were deemed by the committee as a whole to outweigh the advantages to be gained by the movement in giving it a certain colour of legality, which, it was admitted, was before all things desirable to prevent the return

of the reaction.   To this end men were wanted at
the helm of affairs, and to effect a control over them,
whose principles and whose courage were alike
beyond suspicion ; hence the " Secret Directory "
decided that the insurgents in Paris should elect a
provisional authority to which the government of
the nation should be confided, until such time as
it was possible to put the Constitution of '93 into
force.   The question of the form this provincial
government should take in a narrower sense still
remained to be decided.   Debon and Darthé proposed the dictatorship of one man.   In support
of their ideas, the inevitable examples from Roman
history were put forward by them, while they
drew a warning as to the disastrous results of
divided councils from the divisions in the late
Committee of Public Safety during the Terror.
However, the proposition was not favourably
received by the committee as a whole, and so it
was decided that the provisional government
should consist of a committee with a limited
number of members.   The conspirators met
nearly every evening in the house where Babeuf
was concealed.   Babeuf himself was formally
recognised as the leader of the movement, with
whom was deposited the documents and the
correspondence of the organisation and the official
seal of the conspiracy, which bore the words
" Salut Publique " on the border, and with which

every important document had to be stamped before transmission to the revolutionary agent for whom it was destined. The following is given by Buonarroti as the usual agenda of the meetings :—1. Reports of agents, and replies thereto. 2. Documents to be printed. 3. Propositions on the form of the insurrection. 4. The tendency of the legislation to be followed. 5. The institutions and organisation of the Republic. Decisions were taken by a simple majority, and were consigned to a register, in which, however, no signatures appeared.

To this period probably belongs the following draft of a Constitution found amongst the papers seized in connection with the conspiracy. The two decrees there given are interesting, as affording us a glimpse, the second especially, into the ulterior programme of the movement.

The documents in question each bear the heading—" Equality, Liberty, Universal Well-being."

" Considering that the people has long been lulled with empty promises, and that it is time at last to set to work actively on behalf of its welfare, the only object of the revolution :

" Considering that the majestic insurrection of this day shall once for all make an end of want, the constant source of all oppression, the Insurrectionary Committee of Universal Welfare orders as follows :—

" I. On the success of the insurrection, those

poorer citizens whose present habitations are ·in-·sufficient shall not return again to their old places of abode, but shall be quartered immediately in the houses of the conspirators [by 'conspirators' is understood here the parties actually in power]:

" II. The furniture of the above-mentioned rich shall serve the purpose of providing the *sans-culottes* with sufficient household effects :

" III. The revolutionary committees of Paris are empowered to take the necessary steps for the immediate and accurate carrying out of the above decree."·

The draft of another decree, bearing the same motto and superscription, ordains as follows :—

" I. A great national community of goods shall be established in the republic. A national community of goods comprises the following objects : Such property as has been declared national property, and which was not yet sold on the 9th of Thermidor, year II. : II. Such effects of the enemies of the revolution, according to the decrees of the 8th and 13th Ventose of the year II., as were reserved to the poor ; such as, in consequence of a judicial decision, have accrued to the republic, or as shall do so later on ; buildings at present used for public services ; such property as before the law of 1793 belonged to the communes ; such property as appertains to hospitals, or to public educational institutions ; such effects as have been voluntarily given to the republic by their proprietors; the property of those who have enriched themselves in administering public functions; lands left uncultivated by their proprietors: III. The right of inheritance is abolished; all property at present belonging to private persons on their death falls to the national community of goods: IV. As existing property owners, the children of a living father, who have not been called to the army as by law ordained, shall also be reckoned: V. Every French citizen, without distinction of sex, who shall surrender all his possessions in the country, and who devotes his person and work of which he is capable to the country, is a member of the great national community: VI. All who have passed their 16th year, as well as all who are weak in health, in so far as they are poor, are *ipso facto* members of the national community: VII. Young persons placed in the national educational institutions are also members of this community: VIII. The property belonging to the national community shall be exploited in common by all its healthy members: IX. The great national community guarantee to all its members an equal and moderate existence; it will furnish them with all that they require: X. The republic invites all its citizens, by the voluntary surrender of their possessions to the community, to contribute to the success of this reform: XI. From [date not given] no person may hold civil or military office who is not a member of the community :   XII. A great national community of goods shall be administered by locally elected officers, according to the laws, and under the direction of the supreme administration."

A section follows on " public works," containing the following articles :—

" I. Every member of the community is pledged to perform all labour of which he is capable in agriculture and in industry : II. Those are excepted who have passed their sixtieth year, as also the weak in health : III. Those citizens who, in consequence of the voluntary surrender of their possessions, have become members of the national community, will not be compelled to any coarse labour if they have passed their fortieth year, and have practised no handicraft before the publication of this decree : IV. In every community the citizens shall be divided into classes, of which so many shall be formed as there are useful callings ; each class shall comprise all persons carrying on the same calling : V. Each class has to elect its own officers from its members ; these officers shall control the labour and see to equal distribution of the same, shall carry out the regulations of the communal authorities, and shall afford an example of zeal and industry : VI. The law shall determine for each season the length of the working day : VII. In every existing communal governing body shall exist a council of elders delegated from the different callings; this council shall advise the executive body, especially as to the distribution, the more agreeable arrangement, and the improvement of the conditions of labour: VIII. The executive authority shall introduce into the work of the community the application of such machines and processes of labour as are suited to relieve the burden of human toil: IX. The communal authority shall supervise continually the condition of the working classes, and the arrangements within its province, and shall furnish a report to the central authority regularly concerning the matter: X. The transfers of workers from one community to another will be carried out by the central authority, on the basis of its knowledge of the capacities and needs of the community: XI. The central community shall hold, under the supervision of the communes, at whose initiative it shall act, those persons, of either sex, to compulsory labour whose deficient sense of citizenship, or whose laziness, luxury, and laxity of conduct, may have afforded injurious example: their fortunes shall accrue to the national community of goods: XII. The foremen of each class shall furnish the storehouses of the community with such products of agriculture and industry as it may be necessary to keep in hand: XIII. As to the amount of this stored wealth, an accurate report shall be made regularly to the central authority :   XIV. The administrators belonging to the agricultural class shall watch over the breeding and improvement of such animals as are useful for nourishment, clothing, transport, and relief of toil."

"*Of the distribution and utilisation of the property of the community :—*

" I. No member of the community may claim more for himself than the law, through the intermediary of the authorities, allows him :   II. The national community assures from this time to each of its members a healthy, convenient, and well-furnished dwelling ; clothes for work and clothes for leisure, of linen or wool, as the national costume demands ; washing, lighting, heating ; a sufficient quantity of the means of nourishment, as bread, meat, poultry, fish, eggs, butter, or oil, wine and other drinks, such as are customary in different districts ; vegetables, fruits, spices, and other comestibles, such as belong to a moderate and frugal station ; medical aid :   III. In every commune public meals should be held at stated times, which members of the community shall be required to attend :   IV. Civil and military officers shall receive the same treatment as other members of the national community :   V. Every member of the national community who accepts payment or treasures up money shall be punished :   VI. The members of the national community should

9

only receive the commune rations in the district in which they reside, except in cases where public authority shall have sanctioned change of residence: VII. Existing citizens shall be deemed to have their domicile in the commune where they are on the publication of the present decree; the domicile of the pupils brought up in the national educational institutions shall be in the commune in which they were born: VIII. In every commune there shall be officials who shall distribute to the members of the national community the products of agriculture and industry, and convey such to their dwellings: IX. The principles of this distribution shall be determined by law."

" *Of the management of the national community of goods* :—

"I. A national community of goods stands under the legal direction of the highest power: II. As regards the management of the community of goods, the republic is divided into regions: III. A region comprises all adjoining departments which furnish nearly the same kind of products: IV. In every region a subordinate management for the purposes of mediation shall be appointed, to which the directing bodies of each department shall be subordinated: V. Telegraph lines shall serve to expedite communication between the management of departments, and the intermediate management and the supreme management." [Crude forms of telegraphy, by means of signalling and otherwise, had already been invented and experimented with (although not turned to general practical account) in the second half of the eighteenth century.   The introduction of the modern electric telegraphic system in general use dates from more than a generation later than Babeuf's time.]   "VI. The supreme management shall determine, according to law, the manner and extent of the apportionment of goods to the members of the different regions: VII. On the basis of these regulations, the departmental managements shall report to the intermediate managements the deficit or excess of products in their several arrondissements: VIII. The intermediary managements shall equalise, as far as possible, the deficit of one department by the excess of another; shall give the necessary instructions, and furnish the supreme management with general accounts of their deficit or excess: IX. The supreme management shall supply the needs of those regions having a deficit by the difference from those having a surplus, or by foreign exchanges: X. Before everything else, the supreme management shall cause the tithe of the total produce of the community to be appropriated and stored in the warehouses of the military authority every year: XI. Care shall be taken that the surplus of the republic shall be conscientiously held in reserve for years of bad harvests."

"*Of Trade.*—I. All private trade with foreign countries is forbidden; commodities entering the country in this way will be confiscated for the benefit of the national community; those acting to the contrary will be punished: II. The republic shall acquire for the national community those objects of which it has need by exchanging its surplus of agricultural and industrial products against those of other nations: III. For this purpose suitable warehouses shall be erected on the frontiers and on the coasts: IV. The supreme management effects foreign trade by means of its agents; it has the surplus which it wishes to exchange warehoused in the above buildings, in which also commodities ordered from abroad shall be received: V. The appointed agents of the supreme management in the trade warehouses shall be often changed. Untrustworthy officials shall be severely punished."

"*Of Transport.*—I. In every commune there shall be officers appointed to superintend the transport of communal goods from one commune to another: II. Every commune shall be provided with adequate means for water and for land transport: III. The members of the national community will be ordered in turn to supervise and carry out the conveying of goods from one commune to the other: IV. Every year the intermediary managements shall commission a certain number of young people from all the departments under their care to deal with the more remote transport of goods: V. The maintenance of the citizen concerned with transport service devolves upon the commune where he happens to be at the moment: VI. The supreme management shall see to it that the conveyance of goods serving to supply the deficit of those regions which are in want shall be carried out as expeditiously as possible, under the superintendence of the intermediary management.

"*Of Taxes.*—I. Only persons not belonging to the community are liable to taxation: II. They have to pay the taxes previously fixed: III. These taxes are to be paid in kind, and to be delivered to the warehouses of the national community: IV. The total contributions of those liable to taxation is each year to be double that of the previous year: V. This total contribution shall be distributed over all persons liable to taxation, progressively, on an ascending scale, according to the department: VI. Non-members of the community may, in case of need, be required to advance the surplus of the necessaries of life and the products of industry, on account of future taxes, and deliver them into the warehouses of the national community.

"*Of Debts.*—I. The national debt is extinguished for all Frenchmen: II. The republic will reimburse to foreigners the capital value of the funds it owes them. Until this is done it will continue to pay interest on the loans contracted by it, also annuities payable to foreigners: III. The debts of every Frenchman who is a member of the national community towards another Frenchman are annulled: IV. The republic shall assume the responsibility for the debts of members of the community towards foreigners: V. Every fraud in this respect shall be punished with penal servitude for life.

" *Of Finance.*—I. The republic coins no more money: II. Such money as accrues to the national community shall be utilised for the purpose of purchasing commodities required by the community from foreign nations: III. Every individual not belonging to the community who is convicted of having offered money to one of its members shall be severely punished: IV. Neither gold nor silver shall be in future imported into the republic."

The foregoing document, which was never more than a draft, may or may not have been drawn up by Babeuf himself. In any case it is instructive, as illustrative of the notions of socialistic reorganisation held by the most clear-thinking heads of the party of Equals, and not less of eighteenth-century sociology in general. The common fallacy inherent in the latter, and in which the Babouvists shared, was the notion that a new society could be voluntarily built up overnight, based on abstract concepts, and finished off in its details, by the artistic sense of a few capable leaders.   What further strikes us in reading the Babouvists' mani-festoes, drafts, and programmes, as in the other proposals and speeches of the time bearing on social reform or revolution, is the comparative simplicity of the economic structure of society before the rise of the great machine-industry, and all that the latter has involved.   As William Morris used to say, the change in social conditions between the first Egyptian dynasty and the end of the eighteenth century was, take it all in all, less profound than the change between the end of the eighteenth and the end of the nineteenth centuries.   The theory of the Equals, as that of their successors, the Utopian Socialists of the earlier nineteenth century, was a scheme of social reconstructiou.   To-day, in the earlier twentieth century, we have done with schemes.   Modern Socialism has no scheme : it has certain principles, and certain tactics and methods of action for the furtherance and carrying out of those principles, but as to the precise construction of the detail of life in the society of the future it ventures no prophecy.   The complexity of modern social conditions and our knowledge of the doctrine of evolution in general, and of its application to historical growth in particular, has taught us the futility and puerility of attempts, however well-meaning, to mechanically mould conditions of life which must be dependent in great part at least upon a complex series of unforeseeable events. To criticise the draft programme above given in detail would serve no purpose. The general sentiment and view of life of the *petit bourgeois*, of the frugal, thrifty, simple-living peasant, small master, or independent craftsman, dominates the whole, as it dominated contemporary revolutionary thought generally. The only point that was new in the theory of the Equals, and that showed a unique foresight, at least in one respect, with Babeuf and his friends, was the notion of the transformation of the entire French republic, by the seizure of the political power, into one great communistic society, thereby anticipating the modern notion of the dependence of organic social change on political means.

CHAPTER VI

THE PROJECTED INSURRECTION AND ITS PLAN

ONE of the most important of the immediate objects now to be attained was deemed to be the adhesion of a sufficient number of the military; and indeed there was some reason for the Babouvists to hope that they might gain over a considerable contingent of the armed forces at the disposal of the government. On the success of the projected *coup d'état*, the people of Paris were to elect a national assembly, clothed with supreme authority, and composed of one democrat for each department, to be nominated by the committee or "Secret Directory," which would not dissolve, but would continue to watch over the conduct of the National Assembly.

Notwithstanding the efforts made to gain over the army, the possibility of a collision with the armed force of the government was not left out of sight. To this end members of the old Jacobin party were summoned from all over France to come to Paris and hold themselves ready for the signal of the insurrection. Lyons was especially regarded by the conspirators as a field of recruitment, and they were in constant communication with the former mayor of the city, Bertrand, who was untiring in stimulating the interest of the Jacobins of the city in the new movement. Meanwhile, in Paris itself, secret stores of arms and ammunition were prepared, and the means of access to government stores were carefully noted.

The government party, on its side, was divided into two main centres, the *nouveaux riches*, the men who had enriched themselves by the Revolution, who had annexed to themselves vast portions of the wealth of the nobility and clergy, and who dreaded equally the return to the *ancien régime* and the ascendancy of those who might be disposed to sympathise with it, and the advent again to control of the State of the popular revolutionary forces. In either case their security of possession was threatened. Among the leaders of this party of the new wealthy middle-class, there may again be mentioned Barras, Tallien, Legendre, Fréron, Merlin de Thionville, and Rewbell—as will be seen, mainly renegades of the old revolutionary party of the Mountain. In opposition to this party, which at the moment was dominant, were the Conservatives, the sympathisers with the *ancien régime*, to whom had rallied many of the old moderates, and notably the former members of the Girondin party, who had been reinstated in the Convention after Thermidor, and who formed a centre of the Conservative block, together with old men of the plain, Boissy d'Anglas, Thibaudeau, Camille Jourdan, etc. On this section of the councils the hopes of the Royalists largely rested. They were prepared, however, as a party, to adopt violent methods if they saw any chance of success in such a course. On their side the dominant faction, the party of the *nouveaux riches*, as I have termed them, did not hesitate, by means of orators and journalists, to denounce all opposed to themselves as enemies of the Republic, confounding in the same category the old revolutionary party, now represented by the Babouvists, and the Royalists, who were openly plotting the restoration of the monarchy, and all it implied. Babeuf had already exposed this trick in one of the last numbers of the *Tribun du Peuple.*

Just at this time, to complicate matters, the " Secret Directory " was confronted with a rival conspiracy on the part of certain members of the old party of the Mountain in the Convention, who had been driven out of the latter body, and been declared ineligible for election to the new councils, and who, it was said, were taking steps to obtain control of the insurrectionary movement. The " Secret Directory " was thus placed in a position of some difficulty. Its members were indisposed to hand over the control to a miscellaneous committee of men, of some of whom the views were doubtful, and others of whom were unreliable in a political crisis, owing to weakness of character. At the same time, the fact remained that these men, all of them, had suffered from being true to the democracy; that they were honest, and that their sympathies at least were in general sound. The Babouvist leaders therefore decided to steer a middle course. They instructed their agents to caution the populace against any movement which might emanate from these persons, and at the same time to circumvent, by warnings and otherwise, any attempts of the government to lay hands on them, attempts of which they were duly notified by their own spies in the ministry of the police.

Meanwhile, the new democratic movement had become so menacing that both of the reactionary parties alike found it prudent to bury their hatchet, and to join forces against the common enemy. No stone was left unturned in the matter of vilification. The leaders were venal, it was said; they aimed at throwing France into a state of anarchy, with the double object of enriching themselves by plunder in the general scramble, and of earning their wages with the Royalists by paving the way for the return of the monarchy. The calumnies were not only repeated at large by the agents of the government, but the executive Directory emphasised them in an official manifesto. Having in this way struck terror into the minds of the timid and well-to-do population generally, but above all into the members of the two councils, on the 27th and 28th of Germinal the Directory laid two bills before the councils, embodying clauses of the most stringent character against the right of public meeting and public discussion. These drastic laws were passed the same day without modification in the Council of Five Hundred, with only a minority of twelve against them, and in the Council of the Ancients with unanimity. It now became practically impossible to carry on the work of propaganda and organisation. The final struggle had already begun.

Such was the state of affairs when the cry went out amongst the democrats that the day had come to live free or to die. But, however, our Babouvists' committee, the Secret Directory, hesitated even now to give the signal for action, as it was anxious to make sure of having all the threads of the movement in its hands before striking. Sufficient discipline reigned in the popular movement itself, combined with a sufficient confidence in the heads of the conspiracy, to prevent a premature outbreak. It was evident now that the revolution would have to be accomplished by a *coup de main*. The design of the Secret Directory was to proceed at once to make an example of the

heads of the usurping power of the executive
Directory (of government), together with the
whole machinery of the illegitimate constitution of
the year III., the opening act of severity to be
followed by an immediate amnesty. It was
decided that on the day decreed for the rising to
take place, banners should be distributed to the
revolutionary agents, and that in the name of the
Insurrectionary Committee of the "Secret Directory" a proclamation should be issued threatening
the death of anyone carrying out an order of the
usurpatory government. Babeuf and his friends
would thus place themselves at the head of the
movement. Finally, after a long and earnest
discussion, the following manifesto was adopted, the
publication of which throughout Paris was to be
the signal for the general rising. It was headed,
" Act of Insurrection" (*Acte Insurrecteur*) and was
as follows :—

" French Democrats ! Considering that the oppression and misery of the people has reached its
height; that the state of tyranny and misfortune
is due to the actual government ;

" Considering that the numerous crimes of governments have always excited against them the daily
and always useless complaints of the governed ;

" Considering that the Constitution sworn to by
the people in 1793 was placed by it under the protection of all the virtues ; that in consequence,

when the entire people has lost all the means
guaranteeing it against despotism, it is the most
courageous, the most intrepid virtue to take the
initiative of insurrection, and to direct the enfranchisement of the masses;

" Considering that the ' rights of man,' recognised
at the same epoch of '93, accord to the whole people,
or to each of its sections, as the most sacred of
rights, and the most indispensable of duties, to
rise in insurrection against any government that
violates its rights, and that they enjoin every free
man to put to instant death those who usurp the
sovereignty;

" Considering that a faction has conspired to usurp
the sovereignty, in substituting its private will for
the public will, freely and legally expressed in the
primary assemblies of 1793, in imposing on the
French people, by means of the persecution and
the assassination of all the friends of liberty, an
execrable code called 'the Constitution of Anno
III.' (1795), in place of the democratic pact of
1793, which had been accepted with so much
enthusiasm;

" Considering the tyrannical Code of 1795 violates the most precious rights, in that it establishes
distinction between citizens, interdicts their right
to sanction laws, to change the constitution, and
to assemble themselves in public meeting, limits
their liberty in the choice of public agents, and

leaves them no guarantee against the usurpation of rulers ;

" Considering that the authors of this atrocious code have established themselves in a state of determined rebellion against the people, since they have arrogated to themselves, in contempt of the supreme will, that authority which the nation alone has the right to confer ; that they have created either themselves or, with the aid of a handful of factious persons and the enemies of the people, on the one hand, kings under a disguised name, and on the other, independent legislators ;

" Considering that these oppressors, after having done everything to demoralise the people, after having outraged, abused, and destroyed the attributes and institutions of liberty and democracy, after having assassinated the best friends of the public, recalled and protected its most atrocious enemies, pillaged and exhausted the public treasury, drained all the national resources, totally discredited the public money, made the most infamous bankruptcy, handed over to the avidity of the rich the last remnants of the unfortunate, who have been for well-nigh two years past dying of hunger every day, not content with so many crimes, have come now, by a refinement of tyranny, to rob the people of their right of complaint ;

" Considering that they have instigated and favoured plots for continuing the civil war in the departments of the west, while deceiving the nation with a patched-up peace, of which the secret articles stipulated conditions contrary to the will, dignity, security, and interest, of the French people ;

" Considering that, quite recently, they have invited to themselves a crowd of foreigners, and that all the principal conspirators of Europe are at this moment in Paris in order to consummate the last act of the counter-revolution ;

" Considering that they have disbanded and treated with indignity those battalions that have had the virtue to refuse to second them in their atrocious designs against the people ; that they have dared to indict those who are brave soldiers, who have displayed the most energy against oppression, and that they have joined to this infamy that of ascribing their generous resistance to the will of tyrants, to royalist inspiration ;

" Considering that it would be difficult and take too long to follow and to retrace completely the course of this criminal government, every thought and every act of which is a national offence, but that proofs of all these crimes are traced in letters of blood throughout the whole Republic, and that from all the departments unanimous cries demand its suppression, it pertains to that portion of the citizens who are nearest the oppressors to attack the oppression ; that this portion bears in trust

10

liberty for which it is responsible towards the whole State, and that too long silence would render it the accomplice of tyranny ;

"Considering, finally, that all the defenders of liberty are ready ;

"After having constituted themselves an Insurrectionary Committee of Public Safety, that has taken upon its head the responsibility and initiative of the insurrection, it is ordained as follows :—

"1. The people's insurrection is against tyranny.

"2. The object of the insurrection is the reestablishment of the Constitution of 1793, the liberty, equality, and the well-being of all.

"3. This day, this very hour, citizens and citizenesses will march from all points in their order, without waiting for the movement of neighbouring quarters, which they will cause to march with them. They will rally to the sound of the tocsin and trumpets, under the conduct of the patriots to whom the Insurrectionary Committee shall have confided banners bearing the inscription—'THE CONSTITUTION OF 1793: EQUALITY, LIBERTY, AND COMMON WELFARE.' Other banners will bear the words : 'When the Government violates the rights of the People, insurrection is for the People, and for each portion of the People, the most sacred of rights and the most indispensable of duties.'

"Those who usurp sovereignty ought to be put to death by free men. Generals of the people will be distinguished by tricolor ribands floating conspicuously round their hats.

" 4. All citizens shall repair with their arms, or in default of arms, with other instruments of attack, under the sole direction of the above patriots, to the chief places of their respective arrondissements.

" 5. All kinds of arms shall be seized by the insurgents wherever they find them.

" 6. The barriers of the banks of the river will be carefully guarded; no one may leave Paris without a formal and special order of the Insurrectionary Committee; no one shall enter but couriers, conductors, porters, and carriers of foodstuff, to whom protection and security will be given.

" 7. The people shall seize the national treasury, post, the houses of ministers, and every public and private building containing provisions or ammunition of war.

" 8. The Insurrectionary Committee of Public Safety gives to the sacred legions of the camps surrounding Paris, who have sworn to die for Equality, the order to sustain everywhere the efforts of the people.

" 9. The patriots in the departments fled to Paris, and the brave officers who have been dismissed, are called upon to distinguish themselves in this sacred struggle.

" 10. The two Councils and the Directory,

usurpers of popular authority, shall be dissolved, and all the members composing them shall be immediately judged by the people.

" 11. All power ceasing before that of the people, no pretended deputy, member of the usurping authority, director, administrator, judge, officer, supporter of the national guard, or any public functionary whatsoever, may exercise any act of authority or give any order : those who act to the contrary shall be immediately put to death.   Every member of the pretended legislative body or director found in the streets shall be arrested and conducted immediately to the police office in his quarter.

" 12. All opposition shall be suppressed immediately by force.   Those opposing shall be exterminated ; those equally shall be put to death who beat or cause to be beaten a *générale* ; foreigners, of whatever nation, who shall be found in the streets ; all the presidents, secretaries, and commanders of the royalist conspiracy of Vendémiaire who shall dare to show themselves.

" 13. All the envoys of foreign powers are ordered to remain in their houses during the insurrection : they are under the safeguard of the people.

" 14. Provisions of all kinds shall be brought to the people in the public places.

" 15. All bakers shall be requisitioned to continue

to make bread, which shall be distributed gratis to the people: they shall be paid on their declaration.

"16. The people shall not take rest until after the destruction of the tyrannical government.

"17. All the possessions of emigrants, of conspirators, and of all the enemies of the people, shall be distributed without delay to the defenders of the country and the unfortunate. The unfortunate of the whole Republic shall be immediately lodged in the houses of the conspirators. The objects belonging to the people left in the Mont de Piété (public pawn office) shall be immediately returned gratuitously. The French people adopts the wives and children of the brave who shall have succumbed in this holy enterprise; it will nourish them and bring them up; it shall do the same as regards the fathers and mothers, brothers and sisters, to whose existence they were necessary. The patriots proscribed and wandering throughout the whole Republic shall receive succour and suitable means to re-enter the bosoms of their families. They shall be indemnified for the losses they have suffered. War against eternal tyranny, being that which is most opposed to the general peace, those of the brave defenders of liberty who shall have helped to terminate it shall be free to return with arms and baggage to their own hearths, where they shall immediately enjoy in addition the rewards so long promised them ; those among them who shall wish to continue to serve the Republic shall be also immediately rewarded in a manner worthy of the generosity of a great and free nation.

" 18. Both public and private property shall be placed under the safeguard of the people.

" 19. The task of ending the Revolution, and of adding to the Republic, Liberty, Equality, and the Constitution of 1793, shall be confided to a National Assembly, composed of one democrat to each department, elected by the insurrectionary people, on the nomination of the insurrectionary committee.

" 20. The Insurrectionary Committee of Public Safety shall remain in permanence until the complete accomplishment of the insurrection."

The intention was, on the destruction of the existing government, that the people of Paris should be called together in general assembly in the Place de la Revolution, where the Secret Directory should give an account of its conduct, and should point out as the source of all its evils economical *in*equality, and, after explaining the advantages which might be expected from the realisation of the Constitution of 1793, should call upon the assembly to ratify the insurrection, after which the provisional government should be nominated by the insurrectionary committee for the approval of the assembly.

On the newly elected Assembly above spoken of being come together, it was proposed to lay before its members the following decree or proclamation: " The people of Paris, after having destroyed " tyranny, using the rights it had received from " nature, recognises and declares to the French " people that the unequal distribution of wealth " and labour is the inexhaustible source of slavery " and public ills; that the labour of all is the one " essential condition of the social contract; that " property in all the wealth of France resides " essentially in the French people, who alone can " determine or change its distribution; that it " orders the National Assembly, which it has " created in the interests and in the name of all " Frenchmen, to improve the Constitution of 1793, " to prepare its prompt execution, and to assume, " by wise institutions, founded on the truths above " cited, unalterable equality, liberty, and welfare " for the French Republic. It enjoins the same " assembly to render an account to the nation, in " one year at latest, of the execution of the present " decree; and finally it engages to cause the decrees " of the said Assembly to be respected in so far " as they are conformable to the above orders, and " to punish with the penalty of traitors those of " its members who shall depart from the duties " that it has prescribed for them."

Such were the schemes which the Secret Directory was elaborating in preparation for the rising. Meanwhile, the propaganda with the military made rapid progress, especially amongst the body called the "legion of police," which was supposed never to be called upon to leave Paris. This it was which specially alarmed the government, the army being the last rampart between them and the deluge. So threatening had two battalions of the "legion of police" become, that in violation of strict legality, the Directory made an order for them to be removed from Paris. This order, which was signed the 9th of Floréal (the 29th of April), was followed by immediate resistance, accompanied by the increase of agitation among the populace. At this moment everything seemed to favour the chances of the insurrection. The revolutionary agents suddenly became more numerous and active than ever amongst the troops. There seemed a fair chance, indeed, of gaining over the whole of the Army of the Interior, as the military forces within and around Paris were at this time called. A committee was even formed in the legion of police itself, in concert with the Secret Directory. Charles Germain was the intermediary between the two committees. A manifesto of the legion was drawn up, prepared for publication. Hundreds of democrats held themselves in readiness; when suddenly the government, annulling the previous order, issued a new one, disbanding the insubordinate battalions. Out of the members of these disbanded battalions, mostly composed of Hébertists, a revolutionary advanced guard was formed, under the auspices of the Secret Directory.

Matters now became pressing; popular effervescence and impatience had reached a point where it became evident to the Secret Directory that further delay would imperil the movement. Accordingly, on the 11th of Floréal (the 1st of May) our Secret Directory convoked some military advisers, to wit, Fion, Germain, Rossignol, Massart, and Grisel, to the last mentioned of whom much importance was attached, owing to the influence he was believed to have in the camp at Grenelle. This important meeting was attended by Babeuf, Buonarroti, Debon, Darthé, Maréchal, and Didier. To the five officers was entrusted the task of directing the military side of the insurrection. They formed a committee which held its first sitting the following day at Rey's, in the Rue du Mont Blanc. Though the military committee maintained outward unity, it was known that the two conventionals, Fion and Rossignol, made no secret of regretting the absence of their old colleagues of the Mountain from the Secret Directory. From this time the meetings of the Secret Directory were transferred to a house in the Faubourg Montmartre. Again, Charles Germain was the intermediary between the latter and the military committee.

Long and earnest discussions took place at this committee as to the conduct of the insurrection. The views of tried revolutionaries from the "legion of police" were heard. One proposition was to enlist the Royalists in the task of overthrowing the executive Directory, but this was at once rejected. Another was by two officers of the legion to poignard that very night the members of the (governmental) Directory, and thus inaugurate the rising. But the want of money at this moment hampered the actions of the conspirators in various directions, while at the same time the question of the old deputies of the Mountain caused much embarrassment. As we have seen, Fion and Rossignol were very dissatisfied at the Mountainist committee being left out in the cold. Much discussion took place in the Secret Directory upon this question, Germain counselling concessions. An amalgamation of the two committees was out of the question.

On the 15th of Floréal, Germain brought to the Secret Directory a delegate from the Mountainist Committee, Ricord. The whole situation was explained to him, the "Act of Insurrection," already given, was handed to the Mountainist deputy to read, and a discussion was entered into concerning the modifications to be made, especially in the article respecting the provisional authority. It was agreed that the old Mountainists of the Convention should form part of the supreme power, but only on condition of their giving irrefragable guarantees of the purity of their democratic aims.

The conditions as agreed to finally between Ricord and the Secret Directory were:—1. The reinstatement of the sixty proscribed Mountainist members of the National Convention in the governing body, which was to consist, in addition, as provided for in the Act of Insurrection, of one democrat for every department, to be elected by the people, on the nomination of the Secret Directory. 2. The dispositions of article 18 of the Act of Insurrection to be carried out without reserve and immediately. 3. The decrees issued by the people of Paris on the day of insurrection to be submitted to. 4. The suspension of all laws and ordinances made since the 9th of Thermidor, year II. 5. The expulsion of all the returned emigrants. Ricord, who accepted these conditions, then left to submit them to his colleagues of the Mountainist committee. The next day he returned to announce their rejection of the terms offered. What they required was in effect the reinstallation, on the success of the insurrection, of the sixty proscribed deputies of the Mountain, without any guarantees or conditions whatever. The addition of a democrat for every department was rejected by the proscribed deputies as a violation of the national sovereignty, which they claimed, under the existing circumstances, resided in their own body alone. The rejoinder of the Secret Directory to this response was interesting:—" In agreeing to the provisional re-establishment of a part of the Convention, we only seek to serve the people. The only recompense to which we aspire is the complete triumph of Equality. We shall fight and expose our lives to give back to the people the fulness of its rights, but we cannot conceive that anyone has the right to claim to be generous towards the master of everything. If you really desire to work with us in the great enterprise we have in view, take care lest you put forward propositions and make offers which throw a bad light upon your intentions." This referred to some phrases in the reply of the Mountainist committee, intimating its willingness to satisfy the social demands of the Babouvists, but rather as an act of grace than as the recognition of a right.

" Many of your colleagues have betrayed the confidence of the people, and we should be infinitely more reprehensible than they if we consented to again deliver the people over to their passions and their weaknesses. In order to re-establish the sovereignty of the people, we ought not to employ the instruments which have caused its loss. It is to those in whom the nation expects the destruction of tyranny that it necessarily delegates the right to take the provisional and indispensable measures to this end. We will not destroy an oppressive government in order to substitute for it another equally so. It is well to pardon error, but it would be folly to confide once more the future of the country to those whose errors have lost it. Better to perish by the hands of the patriots who, indignant at our inaction, may accuse us of cowardice and treason, or by those of the government, who may conceivably obtain knowledge of our schemes, than to put the people again at the mercy of those who immolated its best friends on the 9th of Thermidor, and who since then have basely allowed republicans to be proscribed, and the democratic edifice to be demolished."

Ricord again retired to communicate this definitive resolution to his friends. It was on the 18th Floréal (7th May) that Darthé reported to the Secret Directory concerning a meeting of the Mountainist committee at which he had been present, that, after a violent debate, the addition of one democrat for every department, as well as the clauses respecting social legislation, had been agreed to, after strong speeches in their favour from the old committeemen of the Convention, Amar, and especially Robert Lindet, both of whom strongly championed the position taken up by the Secret Directory. The news of the *entente* between the two organising bodies was immediately communicated to the agents of Babeuf and his colleagues, and renewed activity was shown in hastening on the crisis.

There were now three bodies concerned in organising the insurrection—the Mountainist Committee, the Secret Directory, and the Military Committee appointed by the latter. The arrangements proposed by the Military Committee, and accepted by the others, were, that the insurrection should take place in the daytime, that the generals under the orders of the Secret Directory should lead the people against the enemy, that the insurgents should be divided according to their arrondissement and subdivided by section; that each arrondissement should have its chief, and each section its sub-chief; and finally, that all subordination to the existing authorities should be broken off, and every act recognising their legitimacy punished with instant death. For the final ratification of these conditions and settling of details, a general meeting of the three committees was called together on the evening of the 19th of Floréal (8th of May), at the house of Drouet, in the Place des Piques.

Meanwhile, wholly unsuspected by his colleagues, a traitor had been working alongside of them, George Grisel, of the Grenelle camp, who, as member of the military committee, had taken part in the innermost counsels of the conspiracy. Grisel, it would appear, had for some days been in communication with the (governmental) Directory in the person of Carnot. A written denunciation of the proceedings of the

Secret Directory by Grisel, the 15th Floréal (4th May), exists, in which precise details are given of the latest meetings, notably that of the 11th of Floréal, at which he himself had been presented by Darthé to Babeuf and the others. The traitor, in professing to give an account of the "Act of Insurrection," entirely perverts its sense, depicting Babeuf as a bloodthirsty tiger, enjoining the wholesale massacre of the rich. He emphasises the part played by Drouet in the conspiracy, and discloses the plan of attack against the Directory, the Councils, and the *État major*.

In consequence of these disclosures, Carnot, on the 17th of Floréal, submitted to the Directory a list of 245 persons against whom he wished to issue mandates of arrest, as the heads of the dangerous conspiracy. Amongst the names given were, of course, all those with whom the reader is by this time familiar. The proposition was agreed to by the Directory, and on the 19th Floréal the mandates of arrest were issued. Of those against whom the mandates were launched, thirty-five of them were singled out, amongst whom was Buonarroti, to be brought before the Minister of Police, in order to be interrogated concerning the facts of the conspiracy. Grisel, it should be said, made himself notable for the vehemence of his democratic sentiments, and for the boldness of the measures he proposed. He

was never tired of affirming the devotion of the
soldiers at Grenelle to the democratic principles
animating the movement. The government at
once took steps to execute the warrants. By a
mistake, the residence of Ricord was descended
upon on the 18th Floréal, but no one was found
there. But Grisel's information as regards the
following day was unfortunately only too correct.
As a member of the military committee, he was
able to give the government precise information as
to the place and time of the meeting of the 19th
(Floréal), though, as events showed, owing to
clumsily given instructions, the project of the
government again miscarried.

The meeting at the house of Drouet took place,
and lasted from eight in the evening until a
quarter to eleven. Babeuf, Buonarroti, Darthé,
Didier, Fion, Massart, Rossignol, Robert Lindet,
Drouet, Ricord, Langelot, and Jauveux were
present, and, in addition, the infamous Grisel.
A member of the Secret Directory opened the
proceedings with an eloquent adjuration to those
present in the traditional style of eighteenth-
century revolutionary oratory. The ex-member
of the Committee of Public Safety, Robert Lindet,
also spoke, on behalf of the Mountainists, on the
justice of the proposed insurrection, justifying
the reinstatement of the remains of the old
Mountain, as the Convention insisted on the

necessity of impressing the stamp of the most strict equality upon the Revolution, and of giving it a thoroughly popular character. Grisel then rose. " As for me," he said, " I speak for my brave comrades of the camp of Grenelle ; and to show you how I take to heart the triumph of Equality, I will tell you that I have succeeded in extracting from my aristocrat uncle the sum of 10,000 livres (francs), which I intend to devote to procuring refreshments for the insurgent soldiers." The Act of Insurrection, as amended, was formally approved by the Mountainists, who by their delegates promised on the day of insurrection to repair to the place that might be indicated by the Secret Directory, and sincerely to co-operate in the common work. Massart, in the name of the Military Committee, explained the basis of the plan of attack proposed. The twelve arrondissements of Paris, united in three divisions, should be marched by as many generals upon the legislative bodies, the executive Directory, and the *État major* of the Army of the Interior. The advanced guard was to be formed of the most ardent democrats. He added that the committee required further information of the numbers of the insurgents and of the capacity of some of them ; also as to the places where arms and ammunition were stored, which it would be necessary to seize at the first start-off. The meeting decided that the Secret

11

Directory should hasten the *dénoûment* of the conspiracy; that it should give its agents instructions conformably to the plan of the Military Committee; that it should meet again two days later and hear a final report on the state of affairs and fix a day for the movement.

The meeting had not long been dissolved before the Minister of Police, with a detachment of infantry and cavalry at his heels, in defiance of the law which forbade domiciliary visits during the night, broke into the house, but found only Drouet and Darthé there, whom he did not consider it prudent to arrest by themselves. He accordingly withdrew with his escort. The event, notwithstanding, as might be imagined, at once aroused suspicion of treachery, which for the moment fell unfairly enough, as Buonarroti informs us, on Charles Germain, owing to the fact of his absence from the meeting on the occasion in question,—an absence caused by a prosecution having already been begun against him. But the astute Grisel soon succeeded in explaining away the occurrence, and fatally allaying all suspicion. He used the blundering proceeding of the government in making their raid after the meeting was over, and the fact that they had not taken action at the meeting of the previous week, when they were all assembled at the house where Babeuf was lodging, and where all the documents relating to the movement were kept, as an argument to prove that the raid was not due to any internal treachery, but a piece of official bluff on the part of the Minister of Police to single out old Mountainists known to be disaffected to the existing government as the object of his domiciliary visit.

The insurrection, as represented by the Secret Directory, with the allied committees, had at this moment at its disposal, on a careful estimate made, as Babeuf and his friends show, about 17,000 men, upon whom absolute reliance could be placed. These were composed of the most military members of the old revolutionary sections, disbanded members of the Army of the Interior, revolutionaries of the departments come to Paris to join in the movement, almost the whole of the legion of police, the grenadiers of the legislative body, and the corps consigned at the Invalides ; this formed the nucleus of the revolutionary army. But, in addition, the leaders of the movement, of course, reckoned upon the popular masses of St Marceau and St Antoine, and, in fact, large numbers of the lower-middle and working class throughout Paris, to join in the movement when once set on foot. The desperate economic situation of such, they assumed, must inevitably drive large numbers into a revolt, the first aim of which was an economic revolution that would make an end, not merely of the existing state of things, but of poverty itself, as the inevitable social condition of the majority of mankind.

CHAPTER VII

THE CATASTROPHE

DURING the course of the events described in the last chapter, that is, between the 1st and the 10th of May 1796, it has been proved by recent researches that the government, namely, the executive Directory, together with the Minister of Police, was kept fully informed of everything important that was taking place. We have already spoken of Grisel, the government spy, who was in the innermost councils of the Babouvist Committee, or Secret Directory, as it was called, and himself a member of the Military Committee, upon which the task of drawing up and carrying out the plan of the insurrection devolved. But it would appear that, although perhaps the principal, he was by no means the only agent to keep the authorities *au courant* with the progress of the insurrectionary movement. In addition to the ordinary police spies, of which there were the usual contingent of eavesdroppers, in cafés or elsewhere, where political questions were likely to be canvassed, there were undoubtedly other more important sources of information as to the places of assembly and the actions of the chiefs of the conspiracy.

Among the principal informers was the keeper of the Café des Bains Chinois, which was a rendezvous of the Babouvists and those favourable to the movement. Of especial interest, as regards the relations of the government and the insurrectionary movement of Babeuf and his colleagues, is the question of the part played by Barras, who was the most influential of the five Directors, and the most prominent man at the time. Buonarroti states, in general terms, that Barras had coquetted with the Babouvists, but does not give particulars. In fact, for long the precise relations between Barras and the movement remained in historical obscurity. In a recent work, however (*Histoire et Droit*, 1907, vol. i. pp. 267–293), M. Paul Robriquet has collected evidence of the part played by Barras in the affair, including some unpublished documents in the *Archives nationales*. The next strongest man to Barras on the Directory was Carnot, and between these two men was implacable discord, which culminated later in the affair of the " 18th Fructidor." Hippolyte Carnot, the son of the famous " organiser of victory," in his memoirs of his father, alludes to the complicity of Barras in the matter of the " Equals," thinking that it was only the timely arrest of

Babeuf and his friends that averted catastrophe (*i.e.* from the point of view of the government and the dominant classes). In confirmation of this, M. Robriquet cites a letter he has discovered, signed by one Armand, who was evidently a police agent, to the Minister of Police, containing the words, " I am persuaded that Barras is betraying us, for he has interviews with Rossignol "; and later, in another letter, " the director Barras is more than ever suspect to me. He has had Rossignol informed that he begs the Committee of Insurrection to send him ' a confidential man,' because, says he, ' the moment of the insurrection,' he wishes to pass over to the Faubourg St Antoine with a part of the *État major*," explaining, however, at the same time, that in case the committee does not send him the man he asks for, he would, none the less, " throw himself into the arms of the people."

The same author quotes, further, a letter of Charles Germain to Babeuf, relative to an interview he had had with Barras on the 30th Germinal, anno IV. (19th April 1796). " You ought to know from Darthé or others," writes Germain, " that I was sent for by Barras this morning, the 30th of Germinal. I have had an audience with the director." Germain goes on to give a statement of his conversation with Barras, as much as possible in the language used.

After enlarging on the dangers the country ran from the Royalists, Barras asked his visitor what the patriots thought. " We know," he said, " they are preparing a movement. Good men, their zeal has blinded them ; they are going to get themselves *prairialised*, whereas, in order to save the country, we have got to *vendémiarise*." This, of course, referred to the abortive insurrection of the populace on the 1st of Prairial of the previous year, when the Convention was invaded, but which, after a few hours' triumph, was suppressed, and which led to the expulsion and indictment of the Mountainist section of the Convention for having supported the demands of the insurgents. Barras opposes this to his own exploits, with the aid of Napoleon and his cannon, on the 13th of Vendémiaire, when the Royalist insurrection was suppressed.

Here follows a remarkable utterance of Barras, as reported by Germain: " Like you," Barras is alleged to say, " I know myself that the present state of things is not the end which was contemplated by the men who overthrew the Bastille, the Throne, and Robespierre. Like you, I recognise myself that a change must be made, and that this change is not so far away as some might think ; and when one has the most need of patriots to effect this change, they are meditating our ruin, our death ! They are making themselves, without intending it, perhaps, the instruments of the emigrants, the fanatics, the Royalists, who have ever seen the restored monarchy near at hand." Barras continued, alluding to the pretended complicity of the Babouvists with the Royalists in their intrigues with Pitt and Cobourg, and wound up by challenging Germain to give his own opinion. The latter replied, denying any knowledge of the alleged intrigues with Cobourg, Pitt, Isnard, Robert, etc., but assuring the Director that the people was tired of its oppressors, and would be no more satisfied with a Vendémiaire than with a Prairial, the former having proved of no more benefit to them than the latter. Barras, here interrupting him, expressed regret at not having worked the oracle ("travaillé la marchandise"), if for only three days, in a manner to satisfy the patriots.

He then launched forth into an invective against the Royalists, expressing the wish that the movement might become general and be directed against the Royalists. " I have confidence," he exclaimed, "in the means at my disposal." He then went on to relate that he had lately made an excursion through the popular faubourgs, and that the people all appeared calm and peaceable. " If I had seen anything stirring," he said, " the thing would have been done. I should have marched with the people, for it is by and through the people that, as I hold, the national will manifests itself.

The people," he added, "is not represented by a handful of clumsy agitators." He thereupon renewed his suggestions that the Babouvists should rally round the Directory rather than maintain a secret directory of their own, in opposition to the governmental one. "You cry out," said Barras, "against us, Crucify them! and yet to whom do you propose to attach yourselves? To the Court of Verona! Yes, my friends, it is thither that they want to lead you, whereas that is the very thing we have to kill and destroy. You ought now, my comrade," said he, "to know my mind, my sentiment, and my principles. More than one patriot knows me already; my existence is bound up in that of the Republic and the people. Believe me, that, like all true patriots, I shall neglect nothing for their success; and it is only in order to serve them that I resist my own pressing inclination to abdicate my position, and to retire peacefully into an obscurity which is very dear to me." Barras, in bidding good-bye to Germain, invited him to come and see him from time to time, giving him a *carte de circulation* to facilitate his movements in official regions.

Barras admits in his memoirs that he had received Germain sometimes, but denies absolutely that he had any relations whatever with Babeuf himself, whom, he states, he regarded as a great fool. He naturally was afterwards anxious to excuse himself from the suspicion of having actively favoured the movement of the Equals, but the testimony of others, among whom was Buonarroti, was to the effect that Barras had actually offered his services to "the conspiracy," which certainly seems to be confirmed by the letter above quoted from, and which indeed, even apart from this, might be inferred from the admission of Barras himself, that he had " sometimes received " the ardent Germain. The fellow - director of Barras, Larivellière-Lépeaux, certainly held strongly to the opinion of his having negotiated with the conspirators. "The conduct of Barras," he says, " his relations, his sinister look, his opinions, sufficed to convince us." He also states that this was the opinion of the other directors, and that so strongly were they impressed with the unreliability of their colleague, that the measures to be taken against the conspiracy were only discussed when Barras happened to be absent from the directorial sittings.

That Barras, from what we know of the man, was not actuated by disinterested enthusiasm or regard for principle in his attitude may be taken for granted, though what precisely his "game" was is not quite clear, any more than as to whether Napoleon was privy to it or not. It would seem, however, pretty evident that, notwithstanding the aggressive luxury of his private life, a luxury that had alienated many, as also

the rôle he had played as a Thermidorean, he
thought he might attain an influence with the
revolutionary party by avowedly favouring their
aims on the one side, while playing up to the
representatives of property and the *status quo* on
the other by posing as a man of moderating
counsels. Whether Bonaparte knew of the matter,
and had visions of a forestalled 18th of Brumaire,
and an entry upon the scene as the saviour of
society, as already said, cannot be determined for
certain.

However this may be, and whatever the motives
underlying the attitude of Barras, there is no
doubt whatever of his haste to adopt an " I know
not the man " attitude so soon as he saw the
way things were turning. The moment he was
apprised of the imminent arrest of the Babouvist
leaders, and perceived that the movement was lost,
he made a violent scene with his colleagues, extracting from them a declaration that they had given
no credence to the reports of his treachery circulated by malevolents. At the same time he talked
of appearing before the Council of Five Hundred,
in order to obtain a public satisfaction. Not caring
to show a divided counsel at a moment of peril, the
other Directors calmed Barras, assuring him that
they had no thought of bringing any accusation
against him.

On the 10th of May (21st Floréal, anno IV.),

Carnot, who was president of the executive
Directory, sent a message to the Council of Five
Hundred to inform them that a horrible plot was
to be hatched on the morrow, and that its object
was "to overthrow the French Constitution, to
slaughter the legislative body, all the members of
the government, the *État major* of the Army of
the Interior, and to deliver this great city to general
pillage and frightful massacres." It concluded
with the information that the executive Directory
were informed of the place of meeting of the chiefs
of this conspiracy, and had given orders for their
immediate arrest. The same day, indeed, at the
very moment when the Secret Directory was
planning the final arrangements for the insurrection, a body of soldiers invaded the room where
the sitting was being held and seized the principal
leaders, amongst them being the ex-conventionals belonging to the Mountainist section of the now united
revolutionary party—Vadier, Ricord, Laignelot, and
Drouet. Babeuf himself, however, was not there,
neither was he to be found at his old address,
No. 29 Faubourg St Honoré, but at the house of
the tailor Tissot, No. 21 Rue de la Grande
Truanderie, where the meeting of the 11th of
Floréal was held, and where, as before related, he
had taken refuge as a measure of precaution,
which events proved was ineffectual.

At the moment that the police burst into his

apartment he was engaged in drawing up, in company with Buonarroti and another, the manifestoes intended to determine the lines of the insurrection. All the important papers relating to the movement were seized. In spite of the generosity of the one man of means in the party, Le Pelletier,[1] there was only found in ready cash 2000 livres in assignats. What this amounted to in the depreciated currency of the time is easy to reckon. The poverty, indeed, of the movement threatened to cause its failure, even had it not been prematurely betrayed. Without the co-operation of the military, or at least a considerable section of them, it was impossible that the insurrection could have succeeded; and to ensure the support of the military, it was necessary that they should be paid. It was proposed to divide the insurgent army into three divisions; three generals were to command it, under the order of the general-in-chief. Fion, Germain, Rossignol, and Massart were those designated. All was arranged up to the moment when the tocsin should ring out, and when, at the beat of the *générale*, the popular wards of the city would rise to claim the heritage the revolution had promised them. The arrest

---

[1] This Le Pelletier, it should be noted, was the younger brother of the well-known Louis Michel Le Pelletier de Saint Fargeau, who was assassinated in a café on the day after the vote in the Convention of the king's death, *i.e.* the 21st January 1793.

immediately produced a great sensation on the general public.

The press gave blood-curdling accounts of the projected movement and the objects of the still-born insurrection. Every day brought reports of fresh arrests of the insurrectionists, besides those of Royalists and others. Babeuf and his friends were removed at once to imprisonment in the Temple. All were apparently at first taken to the prison of the Abbaye. This was on the 21st Floréal (10th May). Brought up the same day before the Minister of Police, Charles Cochon Laparent, a former member of the Convention, Babeuf claimed to be the author of the plan of insurrection found among the papers seized. This was, of course, not strictly true, but Babeuf was anxious not to incriminate his associates, whom he steadily refused to name. Two days later he indicted the following letter to the executive Directory:—

"Citizens and Directors,—Would you regard it as beneath you to treat with me as between power and power? You have already seen the vast confidence of which I am the centre! You have seen that my party may well balance yours! You have seen its vast ramifications! I am more than convinced that the outlook has made you tremble!

"Is it to your interest, is it to the interest of

the country, to give special notoriety to the conspiracy and its inspirers? I do not think so. I will give you the reasons why my opinion ought not to appear suspicious. What would happen if this affair should appear in the full light of day? That I should play the most glorious of all rôles! I should demonstrate with all the force of character, with all the energy of which you have known me to be possessed, the righteousness of the conspiracy, of which I never denied having been the ringleader. Departing from that cowardly path strewn with denials, which the common ruck of accused persons use to justify themselves, I should dare to develop great principles, plead the eternal rights of the people, with all the advantage which close absorption and the grandeur of the subject gives me. I should dare, I say, to demonstrate that this trial is not one of justice, but it is one of strength against weakness, of oppressors against oppressed and their magnanimous defenders, of the strong against the weak. You may condemn me to deportation or death, but your judgment will be at once seen to be pronounced by powerful vice against feeble virtue. My scaffold will figure gloriously beside that of Barneveldt or of Sidney. Would you fear to see, after my execution, altars raised to me beside those where to-day Robespierre and Goujon are revered as illustrious martyrs? It is not in this way that governments and rulers are rendered secure. You have seen, citizens and directors, that you hold nothing when I am in your hands. I am not all the conspiracy, it is clear; nay, I am only a single link in the long chain that composes it. You have to fear all the other parties no less than mine. You have, indeed, the proof of all the interest they take in me, that you strike at them all in striking at me, and you will irritate them.

" You will irritate, I say, the whole democracy of the French Republic. But you know already that it is not such a small matter as you may have imagined at first. You must recognise that it is not only in Paris that it exists in strength, you must see that there is not one of the departments where it is not powerful. You would judge of the matter still better if your agents had seized the vast correspondence which enabled us to form the lists of which you have only seen a fragment. It is all very well to seek to stifle the sacred fire which burns and will burn. What though it seems at certain instants extinguished if its flame threatens to revive suddenly with the force of an explosion? Would you undertake to deliver yourselves entirely to that vast *sans-culotte* sect which has not yet deigned to declare itself vanquished? Even in any possibility of this where would you find your-selves afterwards? You are not quite in the same position as he who after the death of

Cromwell ruled some millions of English republicans. Charles II. was king, and whatever you may say you are not that yet. You have need of a party to support you, and if you removed that of the patriots you are left alone in the face of royalism. What do you think would be your lookout if you were standing before it single-handed? You will say that the patriots are as dangerous as the royalists, and perhaps more so. You deceive yourselves. Consider well the character of the enterprise of the patriots. You will not find that they desire your death, and it is a calumny to have allowed the statement to be published. For myself, I can tell you that they do not dèsire it. They wish to walk in other paths than those of Robespierre. They desire no blood. They would force you to confess of yourselves that you have made an oppressive use of power, that you have got rid of all popular forms and safeguards, and they desire you to replace them. They would not have gone as far as they have, if, as you promised after Vendémiaire, you had made the attempt to govern popularly.

" I myself in my earlier numbers [of his paper] have sought to open the door to you. I have said how I thought that you might cover yourselves with the blessing of the people. I explained how it seemed possible to me that you might cause to disappear all that the constitutional character of your government exhibits in contrast to true republican principles.

"Well, there is still time. The turn the latest events have taken may become profitable, and the salvation alike of yourselves and the public interests. Do you disdain my advice and my conclusions, which are that your own interest and that of the country consists in not giving notoriety to the present affair? I seem to perceive that it is already your intention to treat the matter politically. It seems to me that you would be wise in doing so. Don't think that my present action is interested. The open and unusual manner in which I do not cease to declare myself guilty, in the sense in which you accuse me, must show you that I do not act from weakness. Death or exile would be to me the pathway to immortality, and I shall tread it with a heroic and religious zeal, but my proscription, like that of all other democrats, will not advance you one whit, or ensure the salvation of the republic.

"I have seen, on reflection, that in the last resort you have not always been the enemies of this republic. You were once evidently republicans in good faith. Why will you not be so again? Why will you not believe that you who are men have been temporarily led astray like others by the inevitable effect of exaggerations into which circumstances have thrown you? The patriots and the mass of the people have a lacerated heart. Would you tear it still more? What would be the final result? Do not these patriots rather deserve that, instead of aggravating their wounds, you should think at last of curing them? You have, when it pleases you, the initiative of well-being, since in you resides the whole force of public administration. Citizen Directors, govern popularly! Such is all these patriots ask of you! Speaking thus for them, I am sure that they will not interrupt my voice. I am sure of not being repudiated by them. I see but one policy that it is wise for you to take. Declare that there has never been any serious conspiracy. Five men, in thus showing themselves great and generous, can to-day save the country. I allege still further that the patriots will cover you with their bodies, and that you will have no more need of entire armies to defend you. The patriots do not hate you; they only hate your unpopular acts. I will then give you, on my own account, a guarantee as extended as is my habitual frankness. You know the measure of influence that I have with this class of men—I refer to the patriots. Well, I will employ it to convince them that if you are at one with the people, they ought to act at one with you. It would not surely be an unhappy thing if the effect of this simple letter were to pacify the internal condition of France in checking the notoriety of which this affair is the subject. Would it not, at the same time, check all that now opposes itself to the calm of Europe?

" G. BABEUF."

This letter, not perhaps very wise or altogether dignified under the circumstances, had, as might be expected, no effect on its recipients. Four of the Directors at least were uncompromising in their determination mercilessly to stamp out the movement, while the fifth, Barras, whatever may have been his private ideas or inclinations, found himself already an object of secret suspicion to his colleagues, and had to fall in with their projects, with all the alacrity he could assume, if he was to avoid placing himself in a false, and even a dangerous, position. The president of the Directory, Carnot, that "organising genius," carried everything before him at this juncture by his energy and determination. His struggle with the only other man of real ability at the head of affairs, Barras, was deferred to a later day. Barras won on the 18th Fructidor, though only himself to be overthrown by Bonaparte on the 18th Brumaire.

But, to return to our prisoners, they were all at first interned in the Abbaye, three days later to be brought up before the Directors and Jury of the department of Paris. But the Government took an early opportunity of transferring the more important of the prisoners, amongst them Babeuf and

Buonarroti, to the prison of the Temple. One important prisoner, however, was allowed to remain at the Abbaye. We refer to Jean Baptiste Drouet, whose name has been several times mentioned in connection with the proceedings of the Secret Directory. Drouet had a special significance as being a Mountainist member of the Convention, and one of the few who succeeded in getting into the new Council of Five Hundred. It was he who was the postmaster at the small town of Ste. Menehould, and who procured the arrest of Louis XVI. at the time of his flight to Varennes in June 1791. He was a man whose past gave him influence with all the existing parties, and his adhesion to the movement of Babeuf obtained for him additional importance.

Now this man Drouet, in his capacity of political prisoner, was rather a white elephant to the executive Directory. In the first place, his being among the accused prevented the great trial coming under the jurisdiction of the High Court of Justice of Paris, as in the ordinary course it would have done. For by article 265 of the Constitution of the year III. it was provided that members of the Legislature were not to be tried before the ordinary tribunals, but that a special high court was to be established to deal with their cases. Hence it was that the government decided that the whole process should take place before a special high court, whose seat was fixed at the town of Vendôme, in the department of the Loir et Cher. But, for reasons of his own, Barras was particularly unwilling that Drouet should be brought to trial at all. Hence, shortly before the time of the trial came on, on the 1st Fructidor, ann. IV. (17th August 1796), Drouet was allowed, it has now been proved, with the connivance of Barras, to effect his escape from the Abbaye. Drouet succeeded in getting away from France into Switzerland. From thence he went to Teneriffe, where he took a leading part in the successful resistance to the attack of Nelson in the following year. He became a sub-prefect under the Empire, and died at Mâcon in 1824.

On the 9th Prairial, ann. IV. (26th May 1796), the old members of the Society of the Pantheon, together with some of the Mountainists, attempted to raise the populace to deliver the prisoners. The attempt, however, was a failure. During the earlier period of his detention in the Temple, Babeuf's enthusiasm for the cause seemed at times to render him indifferent to every other consideration, even to the welfare of his wife and family. As the weeks went on, however, he softened, and the following letter to his well-to-do friend Felix Le Pelletier is of interest, as expressing at once his political testament and his regard for the domestic affections, and, lastly, as a specimen of his literary style at its

best. It is dated—" The Tower of the Temple,
26th Messidor, anno IV. (10th of August 1796),"
and is as follows :—

." Greetings, dear Felix ! Don't alarm yourself
on seeing these lines traced by my hand. I know
that all that bears the imprint of relations with
me gives the right to disquietude. I am the being
that all fly from ; that all regard as dangerous,
and of a deadly approach. However, my conscience
tells me that I am pure ; and my true friends, that
is, certain just men, know also that I have nothing
wherewith to reproach myself. If even they shun
me, it is not from any real aversion which I inspire
in them, but it is the effect of the factitious terror
imposed upon them by malice, lest by chance they
should be reputed criminals, and treated as such.
In this position the consideration that I owe to
good men prescribes to me the interdiction of all
intercourse with them, in order to avoid giving
them the smallest alarm. But urgent considerations, such as present themselves naturally to the
thoughts of a man on the brink of the tomb, have
decided me to make one more advance towards one
of my fellow-citizens whom I especially esteem. I
do this the more willingly inasmuch as I am sure
to run no other risk than that, perhaps, of somewhat
disquieting him. It is a sacrifice that friendship
can make. I shall lighten it in reassuring you,
as quickly as possible, my good Felix, that there is

nothing to fear. I was certain, in getting this epistle conveyed to you, the last that I shall address to you, that it would overcome without peril all the obstacles that might come between you and me.

"Behold us, then, without doubt, more at ease with one another—you to read me, I to conclude what I have to tell you! I have built my text, in speaking to you, on friendship. I have called you friend! I have believed, and I believe, that I may do so. It is by this title that I address you in confidence—respecting do you know what? —my testament, and last recommendation.

"I make the following assumptions subordinate to its execution—that proscription will not always pursue you; that the tyrants, sated with my blood and that of some of my unhappy companions, will be contented, and their own policy will not counsel them, perhaps, to do what they at first appeared to propose doing, namely, to make a hecatomb of all republicans. On the other hand, it might still happen, after my martyrdom, that fortune will tire of striking our country, and then that her true children may breathe in peace. If it is otherwise, I lose all hope as to what shall survive me. Then all will perish in the vast cataclysm that crime against virtue and justice will engender. The work of the good, their memory, their families, will fall into eternal night, and be involved in one universal destruction. Then, again, all is said.: I need take no more care for those who are still dear to me, whom my thought has followed up to the repose of nothingness, the last inevitable end of all that exists.

" It is on the first supposition that I am acting, my friend. I believe I have remained worthy of the esteem of men who are as just as you are. I have not seen you in the ranks of those evil Machiavellian politicians who multiply my sufferings a hundredfold, and are looking forward to my death. The traitors! In causing those for whom they appeared to have interested themselves most to appear in a cowardly and shameful light, they have pictured me—whose every public act has testified to the rectitude, to the purity of my intentions; to me, whose sighs and tenderness ever for unfortunate humanity are painted in unequivocal traits!—me, who have worked with such courage and devotion for the enfranchisement of my brothers!—me, who in this sublime enterprise have had at the moment of misfortune, following on the great success which attests that I have at least brought some intelligence to the work before me!—they have pictured me, I say, either as a miserable dreamer in oblivion, or as a secret instrument of the perfidy of the enemies of the people. They have not blushed to agree with the tyrants as to the culpability of the most

generous efforts to break down slavery and to
cause the horrible misery of the country to cease.
They have not blushed, finally, to seek to cast
upon me alone this capital offence, in ornamenting
it with all the accessories by which they thought
to be able effectively to give it the colour of
crime ; and, nevertheless, I myself had the delicacy
to compromise no one by name, only involving
in the charge brought against me the coalition of
all the democrats of the entire Republic, because
I thought it at first useful to strike at despotism
with terror, and because I thought it would be
an insult to any democrat not to present him as
a participant in an enterprise so obligatory for
him as that of the re-establishment of equality !
What have they gained, these false brothers, these
apostates from our holy doctrine ?   What have
they gained by this evil system which they appear
to regard as the *non plus ultra* of cleverness?   They
have gained nothing beyond dishonour to themselves, to discredit revolutionaries with the people,
who necessarily always disperse when they see
themselves abandoned by their leaders.   They
have also succeeded in encouraging the enemy by
the spectacle of such weakness.   They have
succeeded, finally, in precipitating the more rapidly
their own protégés into the abyss.   You have not
taken part in these turpitudes, my friend.   You
have already begun to render to us the tribute

of homage, which a just posterity will pay in full."

The letter then proceeds to exculpate Le Pelletier still further from any share in the base conduct of others, and to recall his loyal expressions of devotion to the cause, and to those who were now in prison as its martyrs. Babeuf continues, that to a man who has spoken and who thinks thus, he has no hesitation in addressing the appeal for himself and his family, which forms the concluding portion of the letter.

" I have no need," writes Babeuf, " to assure you, that, in my complete devotion to the people, I have not thought of my personal affairs, neither have I ever forecast as to what might happen in the case of the failure that has now befallen me. I leave two children and a wife, and I leave them without a cent, without the means of livelihood. No! for a man like Felix, it will certainly not be too onerous a legacy to impose upon him, to charge him to aid these unhappy creatures in not dying of want. The daughter of Michel Le Pelletier [the before-mentioned murdered member of the Convention] will assist in this worthy work; her character, that I have had the opportunity of observing, her unmistakable sensibility, already accustomed to exercise itself towards those unfortunates that the world has made, assure me of all her movements, and of her resolution when you cause her to read this letter. You will permit me to give a little more in detail what I wish to be done for the unfortunates that I am abandoning. My two sons: the elder, as far as I can judge from the little that has been done for his education, will not have a great aptitude for the sciences. This would seem also to argue that he will not have the ambition to play any important rôle in the political arena. Hence he may pass his life quietly, and thus avoid the painful lot and misfortunes of his father. This boy has at least an excellent judgment and an independent spirit, the result of all the ideas in which he has been nourished. I have sounded him as to what he would like to be. Workman, he replied, but workman of the most independent class possible, and he cited that of the printer. He was not so far wrong, perhaps, and I desire nothing more than that he should follow his tastes. I can say nothing as regards his younger brother, who is too young as yet to decide anything as to his capacities; but if I have ground to hope that you will do as much for him as for the elder, I am content. Gracchus Babeuf has never been ambitious for himself or for his children. He has only been anxious to procure some good for the people. He would be too fortunate if he knew that his children were by way of becoming some day good and peaceable artisans, among the classes of which society has always need, and which consequently can never be wanting to her.

"As regards my wife, in the face of the fact that she only has the domestic virtues and the simple qualities belonging to the mother of a family, all that will be necessary to preserve her from a pitiable want will be very little. It will suffice to advance her some small sum to place her in a position to undertake one of those minor occupations such as furnish all that is necessary to keep a small family.

"And now, my good friend, I will ask of you one more favour. The nature of my trial and its slow progress tell me that I have still a certain number of days to live before that day when I shall go to sleep myself on the bed of honour, to expiate the acts which render me supremely culpable in the eyes of the enemies of humanity. I can wish, for my consolation, that my wife and my children might accompany me, so to say, to the foot of the altar where I shall be immolated; that will do me much more good than a confessor. Place them, I pray of you, in a position to make the journey, so that I shall not be deprived of this last satisfaction.

"My body will return to earth. There will remain no more of me than a sufficient quantity of projects, notes, and sketches of democratic and revolutionary writings, all tending to the last aim, to the complete philanthropic system for which I

die. My wife will be able to collect them all ; and
one day, when the persecution shall have slackened,
when perchance good men shall breathe again,
with freedom enough to be able to cast a few
flowers on our tomb, when people will have
come to think again on the means for procuring to
the human race the happiness we have proposed
for it, you may look into those fragments, and
present to all the disciples of Equality, to those of
our friends who preserve our principles in their
hearts—you may present to them, I say, for the
benefit of my memory, a selection of these divers
fragments, containing all that the corrupt of to-day
call my dreams. I have finished. I embrace you
and bid you adieu.   G. BABEUF."

It was not until the 10th Fructidor, ann. IV.
(27th August 1796), that Babeuf and his associates
were transferred to Vendôme during the night, in
cages made on purpose, as Buonarroti alleges, to
make of them an exhibition as of wild beasts.
Gendarmes and a strong detachment of cavalry
escorted the vehicles conveying the accused, which
were followed by others containing their wives and
children, among whom were Madame Babeuf and
her son Émile. Three days later the cortége arrived
at Vendôme, the accused being placed in the cells
under the court buildings, to which all access from
outside was severely prohibited. According to

Buonarroti, the evenings were relieved by the singing of revolutionary songs on the part of the prisoners, in which the inhabitants of the town who happened to be in the neighbourhood of the prison frequently joined.

The high court which was to try them was composed of the president, Gandon, and of five other judges, Coffinhal, Pajou, Moreau, Audier, and Massillon. There were, in addition, two supplementary judges, Lalonde and Ladève. The public prosecutors were Viellart and Bailly. The jury was composed of sixteen members, four adjuncts, and four supplementary members. But the prisoners had still some months to wait in durance. At last, after the usual formalities, the trial began on the 2nd Ventose, ann. V. (the 20th February '97), and was destined to drag on its course to the 7th Prairial, ann. V. (27th May 1797).

Meanwhile, the remains of the party of which Babeuf was the leader were not inactive in Paris. Babeuf and his associates had been scarcely a month in the dungeons beneath the courthouse of Vendôme before a final attempt, which had been some weeks in preparation, was made to win over to the revolutionary cause the military in the camp at Grenelle, near Paris. On the 7th of September some hundreds of followers of the Babeuf movement rose in abortive insurrection. Their plan was first of all to seize the palace of the

Luxembourg, the official residence of the Directory, and where the five directors were sitting, and next, after securing the persons of the directors, to proceed to the camp of Grenelle, there to induce a movement among the military, and to bring back those favourable to their scheme as an armed force to Paris.

But the attack on the Luxembourg failed. The authorities, warned in time of the movement that was on foot, reinforced the guards round the governmental palace, and the attacking force was driven off, although not effectively dispersed. The insurgents rallied but did not a second time attempt to penetrate into the Luxembourg. Abandoning this part of their plan, they proceeded in a body to Grenelle. Here they had every hope of success, judging from the reports they had received, but here also they were likewise doomed to a failure that proved the final disaster to their party. On summoning the camp, in which General Latour was in command, to join them, they were greeted with an unexpected resistance, under the immediate orders of Colonel Marlo. Instead of, as they had hoped and expected, tokens of fraternisation, they were met by a series of volleys fired into their number. In a few minutes they were in panic-stricken flight, leaving more than a hundred dead and wounded on the field.

This attempt on the camp at Grenelle was the

last dying flicker of the spirit of popular insurrection in Paris and France for a long time to come, and may be fittingly regarded as the closing episode of the French Revolution, considered as one distinct and connected historical event.

The Government could have wished for nothing better than this abortive demonstration. It afforded them an excuse for hunting down all suspected of revolutionary sympathies in Paris and the departments surrounding the capital. Those arrested soon approached the number of 300. These prisoners were not brought before the ordinary tribunals, but were tried by a specially appointed military commission, in other words, a court martial. As might be expected, numerous sentences of death were pronounced, and as many as thirty persons were executed by military platoons on the plain of Grenelle. In addition to this, a large number were sentenced to penal servitude and to deportation. The only prominent person who had the courage to defend the vanquished democrats was the noble-minded Pache, the late Mayor of Paris, during the period of the first Commune, who issued, from his residence in the country, whither he had retired, a pamphlet zealously championing the unfortunate victims, and denouncing in scathing terms the conduct of the governing classes of the day.

13

CHAPTER VIII

THE TRIAL OF BABEUF AND HIS COLLEAGUES

On the opening of the proceedings on the 2nd of Ventose (anno V.), forty-seven prisoners were brought up, eighteen of the accused being *en contumace*. Among the latter were Drouet, Lindet, Reys, Le Pelletier, and Rossignol. A large force of troops surrounded the building where the trial was held, while each of the accused was guarded by two gendarmes. The place reserved in the large audience hall for the public was always filled with admirers of the incriminated movement, who vigorously applauded every utterance of the prisoners. Many of the accused, it should be remarked, though belonging to the revolutionary movement, had had nothing whatever to do with the actual conspiracy, but were arrested out of spite. Amongst the prisoners present might have been seen the old Jacobin and landlord of Robespierre, Duplay and his son.

Those whose voices were chiefly heard in defence

of the movement were those of Babeuf, Germain, Antonelle, and Buonarroti.

Darthé remained silent, refusing to recognise the jurisdiction of the court. He made one speech only at the beginning of the proceedings, which is given by Buonarroti. "As for me," it is related that he said, "if providence has fixed for this epoch the end of my career, I shall end it with glory, without fear and without regret. What have I indeed to regret? When liberty succumbs; when the edifice of the Republic is crumbling piece by piece; when its name has become odious; when its friends, worshippers of Equality, are pursued, are hunted, scattered, given over to the rage of assassins or to the agonies of hunger; when the people are the prey of famine and of want, deprived of all their rights, abused, despised, crushed beneath a yoke of iron; when this sublime Revolution, the hope and consolation of oppressed nations, has ceased to be more than a phantom; when the defenders of the country are everywhere covered with outrages, deprived of all, maltreated, bent beneath the most odious despotism; when, as the price of their sacrifices, of their blood poured out in the common defence, they are treated as criminals, assassins, and brigands, their laurels changed to cypress; when royalism is everywhere bold, protected, honoured, recompensed even with the blood and tears of the unfortunate; when fanaticism grasps again its poignards, and with a new fury; when proscription and death are suspended over the heads of all virtuous men, of all the friends of reason, of all those who have taken part in the grand and generous efforts in favour of our generation; when, to fill up the tale of horror, it is in the name of all that is most sacred, most revered on earth, in the name of holy friendship, of respected virtue, of honourable probity, and of beneficent justice, of sweet humanity, of the Divinity itself, that the brigands drag desolation, despair, and death at their heels; when profound immorality, horrible treason, execrable denunciation, infamous perjury, brigandage, and assassination are officially honoured, distinguished, recognised, and qualified with the sacred name of virtue; when all social ties are broken; when France is covered with a funereal crape; when she will soon offer nothing more to the horrified eye of the traveller than heaps of corpses and smoking deserts; when the country is no more—then is death indeed a blessing! As for myself, I leave to my family and my friends neither opprobrium nor infamy. They will be able to cite with pride my name among those of the defenders and martyrs in the divine cause of humanity. I claim with confidence to have passed through the whole revolutionary period without taint; never has the thought of a crime or of a meanness sullied

my soul.   Thrown when young into the Revolution
I have supported all its fatigues, have borne all its
dangers, without ever falling back.   I have had no
other pleasure than the hope of seeing the day that
should found the durable reign of equality and of
liberty.   Solely occupied with the sublimity of this
philanthropic enterprise, I have entirely abnegated
myself.   Personal interests, the affairs of my family,
everything has been forgotten and neglected.   My
heart has never beat save for my fellow-men and
for the triumph of justice."

The above harangue, with its characteristic
eighteenth-century ring, were the only words
spoken before the tribunal by Darthé.   The prosecution from the very first gave evidence of the
bitterness of its animus against the accused, as well
as against everything savouring of democracy.
The government prosecutor in his speech conjured
up visions of a faction of monstrous beings hitherto
unknown in the history of mankind, children of
anarchy and crime, to which the prisoners belonged.
To this hideous and diabolical faction he traced all
the democratic episodes of the Revolution; its
whole course, from the taking of the Bastille to the
fall of Robespierre, was involved in one common
anathema.   The government prosecutors even went
so far on the side of reaction as to condone the
royalist insurrection of the 13th Vendémiaire of
the preceding year.   Great efforts were made by

the judges as well as by the public prosecutors to prevent the accused from defending or even expounding the doctrines contained in the *pièces d'accusation*. The outrageous conduct of the court in this matter led to frequent " scenes " throughout the trial.

The vile attempts of these government agents to blacken and vilify the characters of the accused —imputing dishonesty to men who had notoriously risked their lives for the country, and who, unlike their enemies and accusers, the members of the then governing classes, had left the public offices occupied by them, before the triumph of the reaction, in a state of poverty, amounting in some cases to positive indigence—led to many an outburst of indignation from prisoners and public alike. For these men the fundamental principles of the Revolution, as enshrined in the " Rights of Man " and the Constitution of 1793, were a religion, the sacred trust for which they were proud to suffer all things, and if need were to sacrifice their lives. The spirit animating them was shown by the enthusiasm with which they chanted their republican hymns in court each day at the close of the trial.

The chief witness against the accused was the traitor Grisel. Together with him were other police spies, who, however, we are informed by Buonarroti, in spite of their *métier*, were animated by so strong a moral repulsion to the archtraitor that they refused to sit beside him. The defence attempted to get rid of Grisel by invoking the law which made the evidence of a denunciator legally inadmissible in cases where he could personally profit by his denunciation, whether by direct payment or otherwise. The public prosecutors, in order to get over this difficulty, had to maintain that Grisel was not a denunciator "within the meaning of the Act," because, forsooth, his first declaration was made, not to the police, but to one of the Directors (Carnot), a fact which constituted his statements a simple revelation, and not a denunciation in the true sense of the word, thereby excluding him from the category of the law as invoked by the prisoners. Naturally this quibble excited universal derision, but the court, as might have been expected, admitted it all the same. Grisel must be received as a witness at all costs.

There were in all five hundred *pièces de conviction*, consisting of documents seized in the house where Babeuf was lodging at the time of his arrest. The most of them were at once recognised by their authors, though, in a few cases, experts were called in to fix the identity of those responsible for them. Among them were the reports of the agents working in the interests of the Secret Directory in the several arrondissements. The latter documents, which for the most part bear the superscription *Égalité, Liberté, Bonheur Commun*, relate to the question of the state of feeling in the different districts and the persons who might be relied on at the moment of insurrection, to the places where arms were stored, etc.

But here and there flashes afford us an interesting glimpse of the life of Paris at the time: thus (*liasse* xix. 17) in one of these documents, dated in the hand of Babeuf, 8 Floréal, we read:—" Yesterday morning the placard, *Soldier, halt again!* produced the greatest effect in the seventh arrondissement. Among other places, at the corner of the Rue Cloche-Perche, Rue Antoine, more than two thousand readers formed a *queue*. A patrol of cavalry passing by wanted to see what was attracting so great a concourse. The commandant, dismounting, read it through, and was desirous of tearing it down, in order, as he said, to give it his comrades to read. On its being represented to him that he could not remove it without destroying it, he replied, 'In that case it had better be left for the people to read.' He remounted his horse and went off towards the boulevard. Some sought, nevertheless, to pull it down; but a group of readers opposed themselves to this, saying that it contained truth." That a crowd of two thousand persons should so readily collect to read a placard is symptomatic of the excited state of feeling still dominating the Paris populace.

A great fuss was made as to a document containing some words which Babeuf had covered
with a great blot of ink. The discussion on this
subject bid fair to become a free fight between
the prisoners, their counsel, and the court. The
séance had to be abruptly terminated, the prisoners,
as was their custom, intoning a couplet of the
Marseillaise: *Tremblez, tyrans, et vous perfides!*

On one occasion, when the public prosecutors
complained to the judges of the prolongation of
the trial, alleging that a number of voices were
being raised against the dilatoriness of the proceedings in the high court, Babeuf sprang to his feet,
exclaiming, "Whose are those voices?" and, turning
to the public, "You will divine, friends of the
people!" He proceeded to denounce the privileged classes, many of whom could not wait the
ordinary course of law in their bloodthirsty impatience to immolate their victims. In this cry one
would hearken in vain for the voices of the four-and-
twenty millions of oppressed people of whose cause
they, the prisoners, were the defenders. "Virtue
does not die," he concluded. "Tyrants may wallow
in atrocious persecution; they do but destroy the
body; the soul of good men does but change its
covering; on the dissolution of one, it animates
at once other beings, with whom it continues to
inspire generous movements which never more allow
the crime of tyranny to rest in peace. After these

last thoughts, and after all the innovations **that** I see introduced every day to hasten my holocaust, I leave to my oppressors all the facilities they desire; I neglect useless details in my defence; let them strike without reaching anything; I shall sleep in peace in the bosom of virtue."

Grisel related his experiences during two hearings of the court. Buonarroti says that what he stated was in the main true. What revolted everybody was his cynical avowal of treachery and breach of confidence. Turning towards the bench where the accused were sitting, he said, "I only see agents here; not one of them was the real chief of the conspiracy; behind the curtain were men who caused these to work and act." This remark was doubtless aimed by Grisel, who was in the service of Carnot, against the latter's fellow-director and enemy, Barras. The statement, however, called forth from Germain the retort, "If we are too insignificant, go to the banks of the Aube to dig out the sand which covers the corpse of my wife! go dispute it with the worms, less worthy than yourself to devour it! fling yourself like a famished tiger on my mother! add my sisters and their children to your abominable feast! tear my son from the feeble arms of his nurse and crush his tender limbs under your carnivorous fang!" Grisel having referred to the insurrection of Prairial, ann. III., in contemptuous terms, was countered by Babeuf, who, in a harangue redolent of eighteenth-century eloquence, glorified the insurrection and its victims, till the court compelled the speaker to resume his seat. Two soldiers named Meunier and Barbier respectively, who had been condemned already to two years' hard labour for disaffection in the legion of police, were brought up from Vendôme to confirm certain statements made by them in moments of weakness. Far from doing what was demanded of them, they now denied everything. Bowing to the accused, they saluted them by republican songs. They greeted them as friends of the people, demanding to partake in their glory. Their conduct resulted subsequently in a fresh condemnation. Of the five hundred incriminating documents seized at Babeuf's lodging, many were obviously written by his own hand, though some of these were doubtless only copied out by him.

The whole weight of the prosecution bore upon Babeuf. His interrogation lasted during nine long sittings. The attempts to explain away these documents on the part of the accused were naturally successful only in a very limited degree. As Buonarroti observes, their defence amounted to no more than a not very coherent tissue of sophism, which, he adds, they only permitted themselves out of consideration for their companions in misfortune. "The true defence of the accused," he says, "rests entirely in the avowal that they made of their democratic doctrines; in the solemn homage which they rendered to the Constitution of 1793, and in their perseverance in justifying hypothetically the object of the conspiracy." The conspiracy, of course, centred in the formation of a Secret Directory, the object of which was insurrection. It was this "usurpation of the sovereignty," as it was termed, that formed the central indictment of the prosecution. "We have not here," said Babeuf, "a trial of individuals; we have a trial of the Republic itself. It must, in spite of all, be treated with the dignity, the majesty, and the devotion that so powerful an interest commands. All republicans," said Babeuf, "are implicated in this affair; consequently it belongs to the Republic, to the Revolution, to history." He proceeded to thank the genius of liberty for having furnished him with a tribune, even though it were the bench of the accused, from which to declare the truth.

A vehement assertion of admiration for the Constitution of '93, and the denunciation of the illegal violence with which those in power had deprived the people of the rights belonging to them by virtue of it, brought down upon him the intervention of the judges, who condemned him to silence. Buonarroti, when his turn came, justified the existence of the Secret Directory and its manifestoes as in no way contrary to

law or to revolutionary precedent. Babeuf subsequently returned to the charge, proclaiming
at the top of his voice " the awakening of the
true people, the reign of happiness, the reign of
equality and liberty, abundance for all, equality
and liberty for all, the happiness of all — such
are the aims of these pretended conspirators,
who have been painted in such horrifying colours
before the eyes of all France ! "   He justified
the revolutionary principle of the sacred right of
insurrection, repudiating with energy the whittling
away of this principle by the prosecution with
the specious sophism that insurrection is only
legitimate when it is made by the universality of
the citizens, such being obviously equivalent to
the assertion that it was never justified.   On some
of his colleagues, notably Ricord, seeking to throw
the responsibility for certain of the most aggressive
manifestoes on the *agents provocateurs* of the
government, Grisel's name being mentioned in
connection with the " Insurrectionary Act," Babeuf
indignantly spurned this cowardly method of
defence by shamefaced denial and falsehood.
Turning to Ricord, " No ! " he exclaimed, " Grisel
did not do it.   It is not a piece which need
make its author blush, and Grisel is too great a
scoundrel to have drawn up any such document."
Buonarroti, when his turn came to speak, detailed
his career since the dawn of the Revolution,

defended the Constitution of 1793, and denounced the usurping government based on that of the year III.

As the trial went on, day by day, the interest of the public in the proceedings and the sympathy shown with the prisoners grew rather than abated. It had its echo outside the walls of the court-house in an abortive attempt to induce a mutiny in their favour on the part of the soldiers placed on guard at the tribunal. A plot was formed for the escape at least of those most seriously compromised. Suitable tools were smuggled into the prison, by the aid of which a large breach in one of the walls was made. The moment for escape had actually arrived when, through the careless conduct of one of the accused, suspicion was aroused with the authorities, the plan discovered, and all hope of flight was at an end.

Meanwhile, the public prosecutors demanded the guillotine for sundry of the prisoners, while their task in demonstrating at once the reality and gravity of the conspiracy was an easy one, given the mass of incriminatory material. The accused, on their side, for the most part took the line of defence that, even if there had been a conspiracy, it was justified by the fact that the Constitution, against which it was admittedly directed, was itself illegal, being contrary to the will of the people, by which it had never been ratified, and subversive of that will, inasmuch as it abrogated the Constitution of 1793, which, on its side, had been solemnly accepted by the popular voice. In a word, they argued that the existing government, and the constitution on which it was based, was null and void, having no claim on the allegiance of French citizens. The attempt to overthrow it, therefore, so far from being a crime, was rather the assertion of legality against usurpation.

The public prosecutors refused to enter into this question of right and justification, confining their speeches to a demonstration of the facts which could not effectively be denied. They could show without difficulty that there had been a conspiracy, which aimed at subverting the government and at overthrowing the existing economic bases of society. Beyond this, it only remained for them to paint in vivid terms the horrors of anarchy, bloodshed, and general destruction which would have ensued on the success of the conspirators, whose characters and intentions were, of course, blackened by suitable calumnies. The conclusion drawn was, that the equality and popular sovereignty aimed at by the prisoners must inevitably lead, through anarchy, to the return of a king.

The prosecution demanded that the jurors should be limited to examining the question of fact, whether there had really been an attempt to destroy the Constitution of the year III., and that all questions

as to its justification should be ruled out. This
view was, of course, adopted by the court, but
its adoption did not prevent the prisoners from
developing their own principles and their full
consequences to the jury, including a drastic indictment of the authors of the Constitution of the
year III., which placed full power in the hands of
an oligarchy, with the dictatorship of a co-opted
committee at its head. These expressions of
opinion the judges found it impossible to suppress.
In championing the cause of the popular Constitution of 1793, the accused were careful to
expose the trick by which the governing classes,
the authors of the Constitution of the year III.,
which supplanted it, had endeavoured to get public
opinion on their side in attempting to tar it and
all revolutionary principles with the responsibility
for the excesses of the government of the Terror.

"You are always recalling," said they (through
the mouth of Babeuf), "the measures of 1793, but
you pass over in silence all that preceded the
unhappy necessity that originated them. You
forget to remind France of the innumerable
treacheries which caused thousands of citizens to
perish; you forget to speak of the alarming progress of the war in La Vendée, of the liberation of
our frontiers, of the defection of Dumouriez, and of
the revolting protection found for him in the very
heart of the Convention itself; you forget to recall

the unheard-of cruelties by which the barbarous Vendéans tore to pieces and put to death with the most refined torments the defenders of the country and all of those who retained some attachment to the Republic.   If you invoke the shades of the victims of a deplorable severity brought about by the ever-growing dangers of the country, we shall exhume the corpses of the Frenchmen strangled by the counter-revolutionaries at Montauban, at Nancy, at the Champs de Mars, in La Vendée, at Lyons, at Marseilles, at Toulon.   We shall awaken the shades of the millions of republicans mowed down at our frontiers by the partisans of that tyranny for the return of which they ceaselessly conspired, even in the bosom of France itself; we shall pour into the balance the blood shed by your friends in cold calculation with that which the patriots have caused to flow, with regret, in the urgency of defence and in the exaltation of the love of liberty.   Is it us or is it liberty that the national accusers have charged themselves to prosecute?   Their infatuation will not be useless to us, and the jurors will discover, doubtless, in the partiality of the pictures they draw, in the affectation with which they distort history, and in the zeal with which they heap on the heads of the accused acts to which the latter are total strangers, that secret hatred which the enemies of the Republic, cleverer than ourselves, have vowed to its intrepid and too confident defenders."

14

One and all of the prisoners gloried in their affection for the Constitution of the year 1793, as guaranteeing to the people the inalienable right of making its own laws, and for its having been accepted with all but unanimity by the French people.   So conclusive was the logic of the defence that it did not fail at certain times to stagger the public prosecutors themselves, who were often at a loss for a reply.   Were they being indicted, demanded the accused, for having called the attention of the people to the violation of their rights that had been practised upon them?   In that they were only making use of that freedom of speech and of the press that even the Constitution of the year III. itself guaranteed to all Frenchmen. While contending that their accusers had altogether failed to prove the existence of the " dangerous and criminal conspiracy " alleged by them, they nevertheless maintained, that had they really conspired to re-establish the Constitution of 1793, they would only have been doing their duty as citizens in fulfilling the oath to be faithful to liberty, to the sovereignty of the people, and to the Republic. Speaking of the communism with which he and his companions were charged, Babeuf boldly reaffirmed the proposition he had often enough preached in the Pantheon Club, as well as in the *Tribun du Peuple*, that private property is the cause of all the evils on the face of the earth.   " By the preaching

of this doctrine," said he, "long ago proclaimed by
the wise, I have sought to rally to the Republic
the people of Paris, tired of revolutions, discouraged
by misfortunes, and almost converted to royalism
by the intrigues of the enemies of liberty."

Babeuf's defence occupied four days. It was
very diffuse in character, constituting an elaborate
vindication of his whole theory and policy. It is
scarcely necessary to say that the scope and intention of the present work precludes its being given
in extenso, or indeed in anything fuller than a comparatively summary analysis. The complete text,
as revised by Babeuf, and left by him for publication,
extends over more than three hundred closely-
printed pages. These, however, comprise most of
the material—proclamations, decrees, manifestoes,
etc.—already given or described.

The many incidents referred to generally in the
foregoing, respecting the conduct of the proceedings,
reached their climax during the twenty-first sitting,
when the President, losing his temper, stopped
Babeuf abruptly with the words :—" Up till now it
is you who have been conducting these discussions.
I declare to you that from this day it will be me."
He expressed his indignation at hearing Babeuf
deny the conspiracy, recalling the letter to the
Directory of the 21st of Floréal (see page 174), after
his arrest, in which he offered to treat with them on
terms of equality, claiming that he was the centre

of the last conspiracy of Democrats. To this Babeuf replied, he only wanted to scare the Government in order to save the Democrats, and convey the impression of a great conspiracy. Babeuf was continuing the discussion when the President again interrupted, and, with menacing gestures, called out, " We have had enough of your speeches, considering that you now say you only took a secondary part in the movement. Who were, then, the real instigators of the conspiracy ? " The answer of Babeuf to this question was, that the moment had not yet arrived for him to give that explanation. This question of the President was not warranted by the facts, because throughout the proceedings Babeuf never shrank from the responsibility of the part that he had taken, and in no way endeavoured to foist the blame upon his colleagues ; on the contrary, he did everything to emphasise his personal responsibility for all that had taken place.

These are examples only of the various episodes that arose in the course of the proceedings, and were prior to the actual opening by Babeuf of his defence-in-chief. The indignation of the audience was apparent, and someone shouted, " You have no right to put obstacles in the way of an accused in conducting his case ; and in particular," indicating Babeuf, " in any case his head is here to pay ! " Considerable disturbance was created by the noise and angry exclamations from the accused, who shouted invectives against the judges, and demanded how it was possible for them fairly to defend themselves ?

Although indisposed in health, owing to his long confinement, at the twenty-fourth sitting of the Court Babeuf demanded to be allowed to make an application to the Court. The President demurred, with harshness, saying :—" Are you going to read us all these volumes ?   How long do you mean to take ?" Babeuf replied, " The time necessary to state my defence !" Then he asked for an adjournment for eight days to enable him to prepare his statement, urging that it was impossible to defend himself without preparation. After considerable discussion, the Court settled down ; and order being restored, it was decided to grant a delay of four days. On the reassembling of the Court after a lapse of six days, Babeuf began his speech. He read from a written statement of two hundred folio sheets, and went through the documents forming the grounds of the charge against himself and his colleagues, which were, as already stated, very voluminous, making three or four large bundles. He reminded the Court of the extraordinary length of the Act of Accusation, and said that its length and the nature of the speeches for the prosecution had given to those proceedings such prominence and grave importance, and those documents and the speeches gave so many varied reports of the movement, that it was necessary for him to combat them in detail. He lost no opportunity of making propaganda for the principles underlying the acts brought against the accused, warmly denouncing the corruption and treachery towards the people of those in power. At the same time he did not spare the weak places in the armour of the prosecution. For example, the strong point made by the latter was the attempt of the "Equals," as represented by their Secret Directory, to corrupt the Legion of Police. He showed that the latter was already disaffected, quite apart from the agitation of his own party. As a matter of fact, the body called the "Legion of Police" was largely composed of members of the old "revolutionary army" of the First Paris Commune in the Hébertist days, and was rife with Hébertist views. Babeuf claimed indulgence for his prolixity and apparent disorder, and said that an accused before his judges must not be assumed guilty before he had been fully heard, that there was a danger of an apparent show of confusion, which might be mistaken for consciousness of guilt. He quoted the words of Mably, who, writing upon criminal legislation, said, "The first sentiment of an honest man when he is accused of crime is a certain feeling of shame which embarrasses him, and he is momentarily at a loss to defend himself. He dreads the uncertainty of human judgment. It would be monstrous to take this embarrassment for a confession of guilt." He said it would be fairer if an innocent man, when accused, were enabled to calmly justify himself, and present the truth to his tribunal without the embarrassing presence and interruption of his accusers.

"I have dared to conceive and preach the following doctrine :—

"The natural right of men and their destiny to be happy and free. Society is instituted to guarantee the more certainly to each member the natural right of his destiny. When these natural rights are not the lot of all, the social pact is broken. · In order to prevent the social pact being broken, it is necessary to have a guarantee. This guarantee can only reside in the right of each citizen to watch over its infractions, to denounce them to all its members, to be the first to resist oppression, and to exhort other members to resist. Hence the inviolable, indefinite, and individual right to think, to reflect, and to communicate one's thoughts and reflections ; to observe continually if the conditions of the social pact are maintained in their integrity, in their entire conformity to natural rights ; to rise up against their invasion by oppression and against tyranny so soon as recognised ; to propose means for repressing these attempts at usurpation by those who govern, and to reconquer all rights lost. Such is the doctrine solely on account of which I am persecuted. All the rest of what they impute to me is a mere pretext."

Once more we see in the foregoing how the inevitable social compact theory incarnated in Rousseau dominated the revolutionary mind. In this respect Babeuf was no more than the echo of contemporary thought. He continues: "Ah, indeed, we are not the first men who have been persecuted by the powers on earth for holding the like principles. Socrates there was, whose end was the poisoned cup; Jesus, the Galilean, who preached equality of men, the hatred of riches, the love of justice and truth; Lycurgus, who exiled himself to avoid being sacrificed by those whom he had benefited; Agis, the only just one among the kings, who was killed because he was an exception to the rule; the Gracchi at Rome, who were massacred; Manlius, who was thrown from the capitol; Cato, who stabbed himself; Barneveldt and Sydney, who went to the scaffold; Margarot, who vegetated in the deserts; Kosciusko, who languished in the dungeons of St Petersburg; James Welldon, who had his heart torn out; and, nearer home, in our revolution, the martyr Michel Le Pelletier, who perished by the steel of the assassin." Babeuf says further, that it cannot be too often repeated that the proceedings of the accusers against himself and his colleagues were political movements in the French Revolution, and that upon the ultimate issue would depend the standing or falling of the Republic. The royalists, always on the alert, were

vigilantly waiting at all the doors for the results of
the trial. " My name," says he, in effect, " has
acquired a fatal celebrity, as it has been given to
the sect which saw through them all, and had
already devoted them to the poignards. The
epithets, etc., of Robespierrists, Terrorists, Jacobins,
and Anarchists have disappeared ; their place is
taken by that of Babouvists. In the democracy
of Rome I should have been convoked before an
assembly of the people in a public place, and the
people themselves would have been my judges as
to whether I had betrayed them ; but in a great
State like France such a trial is impossible, and the
people cannot constitute themselves a tribunal to
judge those who are accused of conspiring against
them or their accepted Government." Babeuf contended that he and his colleagues could not be
brought within the definition of conspirators as
given by the prosecution in its opening speech,
according to which " conspiracy " meant to overthrow the legitimately established Government, for
they had been unable to show by any of the
numerous writings and documents quoted and
produced against him any elements of such a conspiracy. He claimed that his writings, manifestoes,
decrees, and proclamations contained nothing more
than the precepts put forward by such eminent
writers as Mably, Rousseau, Diderot, Morelly, and
others, who were all tolerated, and were the great

masters of whom he and his colleagues were only the disciples ; that he claimed the liberty of the press to dilate on and review the doctrines and teachings of such great authorities.   Men like Tallien and Armand de la Meuse had advocated the same principles in their writings and speeches, and still remained in the legislative assembly.   Why were *they* not also brought before the High Court ?   And he quoted passages from Tallien's paper, *L'Ami des Sans-culottes*, No. 71, and a long speech of the deputy Armand de la Meuse before the Convention, in which views were expressed such as were common at the time, as to reducing the income of the rich for alleviating the needs of the poor, the result being a tendency to the equalisation of income, or at least to the rendering impossible of anything approaching the extremes of luxurious wealth on the one hand and penurious indigence in the other such as was the usual form assumed by aspirations, towards economic equality during the French Revolution.   Exclaimed Babeuf in conclusion—— "These, then, Gentlemen of the Jury, are the doctrines preached to the conventional assembly by a man who is still actually a member of the Corps Legislatif, and whom nobody ever dreamt of calling a conspirator ! "   The inevitable allusions to Christian teaching followed, with the reminder that these same doctrines brought the founder of Christianity to a similar position to that in which he himself was now placed, and ultimately led to his condemnation and execution as a conspirator. Babeuf refers with dramatic eloquence and sensational warmth to the fact of the arrest of his wife, already told of, which he characterises as an act of "gross immorality" on the part of the authorities, and complains of the conduct of the magistrate or police official who was responsible for that act, and to the petition of the people of Arras to the executive Directory asking for the punishment of that magistrate. It will be remembered that Arras was the town where, with Charles Germain and others, he was retained in prison for a long period without trial. He further goes on to relate to the jury the facts relative to the Bodson correspondence, applying for a fair consideration by them of the above-mentioned document. This correspondence with Bodson, Babeuf maintains, was absolutely confidential, and most unfairly brought forward against him by the prosecution. He says: "Is it not permitted to me to write? Is it not permitted to me, the same as to others, to communicate by letter with whom I wish? Since when have confidential communications in friendship been liable to be delivered to a tribunal, and to be made the foundation of a prosecution?" He emphasises these incidents, and claims that they show the undue severity and harshness meted out to him and his, and to those friends who participated in his ideas, and urges that nothing contained in these documents could be evidence of conspiracy against him ; and if at times he had been violent in his expressions in the articles published in his paper *Le Tribun*, especially referring to No. 40, it was occasioned by the unjust acts of the authorities, which were an outrage on humanity, justice, and the constitution. He points out an important passage in the Act of Accusation which was to the following effect :—

" If these individuals associate together in meetings, communicating their ideas, their wishes, and their hopes ; if they arrange a plan of execution in which all promise to concur ; if each of them charges himself with and fulfils a certain *rôle* ; if the combined efforts of all are directed toward one common end ; if amongst them they establish an organisation, chiefs who give orders and instructions ; if they appoint their agents to carry out those orders conformably to those instructions, there then exists a conspiracy ; it is concerted action which gives it that character ; and this conspiracy is the most criminal of undertakings when its aim is the overthrow of the established government, and the handing over of the nation to the most horrible anarchy.

" Such is precisely the result of the documents that we shall produce. You will see that there was a complete organisation, a constituted directorate, with appointed and empowered agents who had accepted their positions; instructions given by the chiefs, only too faithfully performed by these same agents; an active correspondence between them; a perfectly concerted plan established, all working in accord, that they might more surely arrive at the common end. And what was that end? The overthrow of the constitution, the extinguishment of all legitimate authority, innumerable massacres, universal plunder, the absolute subversion of all social order."

Babeuf reviews this charge, saying:—" I hope, Gentlemen of the Jury, to be able to prove to you that such was not the result of the documents produced. That there was not such an organisation, directory, body of empowered agents, institution, execution, intention, and aim, as pretended by the prosecution." He declares that he had shown during his examination that the organisation of which he was a member was not such an association, but a Club or Reunion of Democrats, who met together for the purpose of discussing the public misfortune and affairs of interest to the country, with the desire and intention of ameliorating the condition of the people, and that with this view they propounded plans and philanthropic schemes of all kinds; that this club was the outcome of the Society of the Pantheon which had been so violently dissolved by the Government, quite con-

trary even to its own law of the constitution of the
year III. Amongst other things, he went on to say
that such meetings of democrats were composed of
malcontents, who had every kind of right on their
side, and such malcontents were warm in their love
of the people. They were not merely republican,
but were partisans of principles superior to the
system of simple republicanism ; in a word, democrats, or citizens who were not satisfied with a
condition of semi-welfare for the people, but who
wished for them perfect rights and independence,
and would tolerate no restrictions of their liberty ;
that these same malcontents, seeing that the
people were far from enjoying the *maximum* of
welfare, the plenitude of independence and liberty
which they believed to have been the aim of the
revolution, fostered a serious desire and hope to
change the Government, which they deemed anti-
popular and contrary to the general well-being ;
that these citizens from the first had put together
and preserved for the public benefit papers containing their views and ideas, their projects and aims
on behalf of the country ; that these papers had
been wrongfully and illegally seized at the time of
his arrest ; that they did not belong to him personally but to all republicans, members of that political
club.

He continued to read extracts from several
numbers of *Le Tribun*, his correspondence with

Germain, Debon, and others, that the prosecutor had endeavered to twist into evidence of an existing conspiracy, and to claim that the jury could not, on fair consideration, find that they contained anything of the sort.

On the fourth day he concluded the reading of his long statement with the following peroration :—

"If, notwithstanding, our death is resolved upon; if the fatal chime has sounded for me; if my last hour is fixed at this moment in the book of destiny, I have for long been prepared for this hour. An almost perpetual victim from the first year of the Revolution of my love for the people; identified with dungeons; familiarised with the idea of torture and of violent death, which are almost always the lot of revolutionaries, what could there be to astonish me in this event? For a year past have I not had the Tarpeian rock ever present to me? It has nothing to affright me! It is beautiful to have one's name inscribed on the column of victims for the love of the people. I am sure that mine will be there! Too happy art thou, Gracchus Babeuf, to perish for the sake of virtue! What, indeed, all things considered, is lacking to my consolation? Can I ever expect to finish my career in a nobler moment of glory? I shall have experienced before my death such sensations as have rarely accompanied those of men who have also sacrificed themselves for humanity. The power which persecuted them has almost always succeeded in stifling for them the voice of truth. Their contemporaries, deceived or terrified by tyranny, have only poured upon their wounds the burning caustics of atrocious calumny and bloody outrage! The thirst of their agony has, for the most part, been assuaged by foul poisons; who knows if, even at the sight of the injustices of the misguided crowd and its perverse seducers, they have not been far from the consoling foresight, that time, the avenger, would rehabilitate their revered names, would ensure for them the worship of every age and guarantee their rights to immortality? At least they had to await posterity. As for us, we have been happier! The power, strong enough to oppress so long, has not been strong enough to defame us. We have seen truth spring forth from every pen during our lifetime, to register those deeds which honour us, and which will redound to the eternal shame of our persecutors. Even our enemies, at least those who are most opposed to us in opinion, even their passionate annalists, all have rendered justice to our virtues. How much the more ought we not to be secure in the thought that impartial history will engrave our memory in honourable traits. I leave to it written monuments, of which each line will witness that I have lived only for justice and the welfare of the people. Who, indeed, are the men among whom I am treated as guilty? A Drouet! a Le Pelletier! O! names dear to the Republic! They are then my accomplices. Friends! you who surround me on these benches, who are you? I know you; you are well-nigh all the founders, the firm sustainers, of this Republic. If they condemn you, if they condemn me, then indeed are we the last of Frenchmen, the last of the energetic Republicans. The fearful royalist Terror which has already so long crushed your brethren, triumphing in your fall, goes about everywhere with its poignards, and a horrible proscription mows down all the friends of liberty.[1] But is it not better not to be witnesses of these last disasters? Is it not better not to have survived slavery, to have died for having sought to have preserved our fellow-citizens? What an abundant source of consolation! Is it not also a source of consolation to have been followed here by our children and by our wives? O! vulgar prejudices, you are nothing for us! Our dear ones have not blushed to follow us to the feet of our judges, since the acts which have conducted us there cannot humiliate either their brows or ours. They will follow us to the feet of Calvary, there to receive our benedictions and our last adieux. But oh! my children, these benches are the only place

---

[1] Babeuf here refers to the so-called "white Terror," the massacres of "Jacobins" in the south of France by the bands known as "Companies of Jesus," "Companies of the Sun," etc.

from whence I can make you hear my voice, since they have taken away from me, contrary to the laws, the satisfaction of seeing you. I have only one bitter regret to express to you. It is that, having desired to the utmost to contribute to leave you liberty, the source of all good things, I see after me slavery, and I leave you the prey of all evils. I have indeed nothing to bequeath to you. I would not bequeath to you my civic virtues, my deep hatred of tyranny, my ardent devotion to equality and liberty, my intense love for the people. I should be making you a too cruel present. What would you do with it, under the royal oppression that must infallibly establish itself? I leave you slaves, and this thought is the only one that will rend my soul in its last moments. I ought, as things are, to give you advice on the means of supporting your fetters more patiently, but I feel that I am utterly incapable of doing so."

CHAPTER IX

THE leader of the accused having terminated his long discourse, observations were addressed to the Court by Buonarroti, Veillart, Massart, Ballyer, Didier, and others. Laflantry, a counsel who appeared for some of the accused, pleaded eloquently on behalf of Buonarroti, and several of the defendants made vain attempts to obtain a hearing, but were cut short by the President, who refused to listen to them. This brought the duration of the trial to the sixty-sixth sitting of the High Court (3 Prairial V.—23rd May 1797), when the President addressed the jury, stating that he was about to put to them three questions which would bring the accused into three categories. The text of the first question of each series was as follows :—

" I. Did there exist in Germinal and Floréal of the year IV. a conspiracy to overthrow the government, and set the citizens up in arms, one against the other? "

227

" II. Did there exist a conspiracy against the legitimate authority ? "

" III. Did there exist a conspiracy to force the dissolution of the two Councils and of the executive Directory ? "

In these were involved two other uniform questions :—

" 1. Who of the accused took part in such conspiracy ? "

" 2. Did he do so with the intention of facilitating the carrying into execution of its intentions ? "

Reypalade, the president juryman, criticised the questions, and particularly remarked as to the law of 27 Germinal, that it had been voted and created expressly to meet the present case and the acts of accusation under consideration. Veillart, in a long speech, appealed to the jury to disregard that law. He submitted that when the jury were convinced that an accused came within only one of the chief questions, they ought to declare that the three must be taken together, and not each of them as capital. One will gather from the above the bias of the Court.

At the following sitting, Rèal, a prominent member of the bar, and one of the principal defending counsel, argued with considerable eloquence against the classification of these questions. He submitted that if they were based on the law of 27 Germinal, as Reypalade had suggested, that the words "*méchamment et à dessein*," which would coincide with the English terms *maliciously, and with criminal intent*, must be added to that of *intentionelle*, or intentionally.

Veillart contested the proposition of Rèal, and insisted upon the conclusions of the day before, and the rejection of the suggested amendments. He was constantly interrupted by the dissenting murmurs of the accused. He was supported in his argument by his colleague Bailly. The discussions which then followed are only of mediocre interest in comparison with those of the opening days.

The defence was exhausted, and the defendants awaited the verdict. As to the prosecution, it was resumed in a virulent harangue launched by the above-mentioned Bailly, one of the national prosecutors. He said, in effect, that the defendants were accused of the most heinous of crimes against the very foundations of French society; that had they succeeded in the objects of their conspiracy, they would have overthrown the Republic "on a mountain of corpses covered with blood and tears." The atrocity of their plans and the extraordinary wickedness of their designs made the ultimate success of such an abominable plot impossible. France was tired of having revolution upon revolution thrust upon her, and so on. He called also to mind the reign of Terror, most disastrous to the State, and the eighteen months of execrable horrors that they had passed through. He said, "Robespierre and his abominable commune have passed away, but all the factions did not go with them. There existed those who would do away with all authority, who wished to have no government, republican or otherwise. And among the journals that agitated such principles was notoriously that of Babeuf, the oft-quoted *Tribun du Peuple*, which, he alleged, advocated absolute disorganisation, and Babeuf, the professed leader of the faction of the pretended ' Equals,' had a preponderance that had astonished all those who had followed the evidence given during the trial. This great luminary, Babeuf, who was their shining light and the very spirit of the movement, and who regarded himself, and was recognised by his colleagues, as the only person capable of directing such stupendous enterprises, this exceedingly hot politician and ardent reformer, now appeared ignominiously before the Court as a very cold and insignificant person, posing as a mere copyist, a servile follower of a small coterie of philanthropic fanatics who dreamt of ways to lead the people to pure democracy."

In addition to the above series of questions put to the jury by the President of the High Court, others were added, relating to alleged provocations, written and verbal, to the re-establishment of the Constitution of 1793. This was done through the mediation, and at the request of the foreman or president of the jury, as just mentioned. In view of the circumstances relating to the constitution of the Court, the violent speech above referred to by the prosecutor Bailly was utterly superfluous, and was simply playing to the gallery.

The proceeding of the Court was, moreover, illegal, as was subsequently recognised by the criminal tribunal of the Seine, which pronounced these questions to have been admitted by the high court of Vendôme in contravention of the law. Buonarroti states that even the public prosecutors did not attempt to defend this action of the Vendôme tribunal against the protests of some of the prisoners, who pleaded that it was a matter suddenly sprung upon the jury, upon which they had not been heard in explanation or defence. But, notwithstanding this, the new counts were proceeded with. The accused laid great stress, moreover, on the form in which the question of intention was laid before the jury. They were much concerned, as already stated, that the adverb *méchamment* (maliciously) should be maintained as part of the questions put, since they specially challenged an examination of the motives which they contended would have actuated them had they been guilty, as the prosecution alleged, of the charge of conspiracy, which formed the chief count in the indictment.

Some of the jurors, of whom there were sixteen, supported the accused, urging legality being
observed in the interrogatories administered to
them. But it was in vain. The judges composing the High Court insisted, as we have seen, on
restricting the conspiracy-indictment to the for-
mula—" Has the accused conspired or provoked,
with the intention of conspiring or provoking ? "—
thus intentionally excluding all reference to moral
justification for the incriminated acts. Only three
of the sixteen jurors were consistently favourable
throughout to the accused. Notwithstanding this,
most of the counts relating to the conspiracy
were met with an acquittal. It was only on the
question of provocation, written and verbal, to the
re-establishment of the Constitution of 1793, that
certain of the prisoners, to wit, Babeuf, Darthé,
Buonarroti, Germain, Cazin, Moroy, Blondeau,
Menessier, and Bouin were convicted. Even
then, " extenuating circumstances " were found for
all except Babeuf and Darthé. The Blondeau
referred to had been arrested for the share he
had taken in attempting to corrupt the guards in
order to enable Babeuf to effect his escape. The
Government seemed to have used this prosecution
as a convenient means of disposing of persons suspected by their agents, or otherwise inconvenient
to them. Thus among the accused was a young
man named Potofeux, who had been lying in gaol

for twelve months, although absolutely a stranger to the Babouvists and their movement.

From the dawn of the 7th of Prairial, year V., the beating of drums, the noise of artillery, and unusual movements of troops announced to the inhabitants of the little town of Vendôme the tragic end of the judicial drama to which they had become so long accustomed. The day the prisoners appeared for the last time before the tribunal the building was filled by a sad and silent crowd. On the declaration of the jury above given, which the eye-witness Buonarroti tells us was pronounced with a voice betraying strong emotion by the foreman, the leading prosecutor rose to demand the penalty of death for the two principal prisoners, namely, Babeuf and Darthé, and transportation for the others. One of the counsel for the defence made a last desperate attempt to get the verdict quashed by invoking the article in the new Constitution of the year III., which declared that no law affecting the liberty of the press should be valid for longer than one year from the date of its promulgation. Hence it was contended that the law of the 27th of Germinal of the year IV., upon which the prosecution had based its indictment, being a law containing clauses contravening the liberty of the press, had ceased to have effect, owing to its having been in existence for more than a year. As might have been expected, the court refused to consider the point, and proceeded to pass sentence on the prisoners in accordance with the demands of the prosecution. Babeuf and Darthé were sentenced to death, and the remaining seven to deportation to the French possessions in tropical America.

No sooner had sentence been pronounced than a violent tumult made itself heard. Babeuf and Darthé had stabbed themselves with daggers. A cry arose, " They are being assassinated ! " Buonarroti sprang to his feet and appealed to the people. The public in the body of the court made a sudden movement, which was immediately suppressed by a hundred bayonets (the precincts of the tribunal were all occupied by military) suddenly appearing and being levelled at the crowd. But Babeuf and Darthé had relied on clumsy, self-made daggers of worthless metal, which broke before reaching the hearts at which they aimed.[1] The only result of their attempt was a night of agony in their cells. For the moment the excitement amongst the public had made itself apparent ; and while the soldiers were in the act of driving back those surrounding the prisoners, the gendarmes rushed forward, seized the latter, and dragged them away to their dungeons, threatening them the while with their sabres.

The following day the two wounded men were

---

[1] According to another account, quoted by Fleury (*Babeuf*, p. 336), their hands were seized by the gendarmes guarding them before they could complete their purpose.

carried to the guillotine. All, even their most vehement political opponents, admit that both, especially Babeuf, mounted the scaffold with a splendid courage that never deserted them to the last. The two bodies were thrown by the executioner and his assistants, according to Buonarroti, into the common sewer, but, according to other accounts, were buried superficially in a plot of land not far off. In any case they were exhumed shortly after by their admirers, and reverently interred in a field belonging to one of the neighbouring peasants. The inhabitants of the little town of Vendôme seem to have deeply sympathised with these victims of counter-revolution. Buonarroti assures us that a deep gloom overhung the town the day of the execution— a "general mourning" is his expression.

During his last painful night, Babeuf manned himself to what must have been the terrible ordeal of inditing the following touching letter to his wife and family:—"Good evening, my friends. I am about to be enveloped in eternal night. I have better expressed to the friend [viz. Le Pelletier], to whom I addressed the two letters you have seen, my situation as regards you than I can do to yourselves. It seems to me that I feel nothing in order to feel too much. I leave your lot in his hands. Alas! I know not if you will find him able to do that which I have asked of him. I

know not how you will be able to reach him.
Your love for me has brought you hither in spite
of all the obstacles of our misery. You have
supported yourself here in the midst of obstacles
and privations. Your constancy has made you
follow all the proceedings of this long, cruel trial,
of which, like myself, you have drunk the bitter
cup. But I do not know how my memory will be
judged, notwithstanding that I believe I have
conducted myself in a manner without reproach.
Lastly, I am ignorant of what will become of all
the republicans, their families, and even their
infants at the breast, in the midst of the royalist
madness which the counter-revolution will bring
with it. Oh! my friends, how agonising are these
reflections in my last moments! To die for the
country, to leave my family, my children, my dear
wife, would be more supportable did I not see at
the end of all, liberty lost, and all that belongs to
sincere republicans covered by the most horrible
proscription! Oh! my tender children, what will
you become? I cannot struggle against the
strongest emotion on your account. Do not
believe, nevertheless, that I feel regret at having
sacrificed myself for the best of all causes, even
though all my efforts should be useless to save it.
I have fulfilled my task. If you should survive
the terrible storm that now bursts over the Republic
and over all that is attached to it; if you should

find yourself once more in a situation of tranquillity, and should secure some friends who would aid you to triumph over your bad fortune, I would urge you to live in union together; I would urge my wife to try and bring up her children in all gentleness, and I would urge my children to merit the goodness of their mother by respecting her and always submitting themselves to her. It belongs to the family of the martyr of liberty to give an example of all the virtues in order to win the esteem and attachment of all good men. I would desire that my wife should do all that is possible to give an education to her children, while entreating all her friends to aid her to the utmost of their power in this object. I beg Émile to pay attention to this wish of a father whom I believe he loves well, and by whom he was so much beloved; I beg him to pay attention to it without loss of time, and as soon as he is able.

" My friends, I hope you will remember me and will often speak of me. I hope that you will believe I have loved you all very much. I could conceive of no other way of rendering you happy than through the common welfare. I have failed; I am sacrificed; it is for you also I die. Speak much of me to Camille. Tell him again and again a thousand times how tenderly I have always borne him in my heart. Say the same to Caius as soon as he is capable of understanding it.

"Lebois has announced that he will print separately our defences. He should give as much publicity as possible to mine. I advise my wife, as my dearest friend, not to hand over to Baudouin, nor to Lebois, nor to others, any copy of my defence without keeping another correct copy by her, in order to make sure that this defence will never be lost. You will know, my dear friend, that this defence is precious, that it will be always dear to virtuous hearts and to the friends of their country. The only legacy which will remain to you from me will be my reputation. And I am sure that the enjoyment of it will console greatly both you and your children. You will love to hear all sympathetic and just hearts say, when speaking of your husband, your father, 'he was perfectly virtuous.'

"Adieu! I am bound to the earth by but a thread, that to-morrow will break. That is certain. The sacrifice has to be made. The wicked are the stronger, and I give way to them. It is at least sweet to die with a conscience as pure as mine. What is cruel, what is agonising, is to be torn from your arms, oh! my tender friends, oh! all that is most dear to me!!! I tear myself away; the violence is done. Adieu! adieu! adieu! ten millions of times adieu!

"Yet one word more. Write to my mother and my sisters. Send them, by diligence or otherwise, my defence, as soon as it is printed. Tell them that I am dead, and try to make these worthy people understand that such a death is glorious, and far from being dishonourable.

" Adieu then, once more, my dearest ones, my tender friends, adieu for ever ! I wrap myself in the bosom of a virtuous slumber."

Fifty-six of the accused were acquitted. Among these was Vadier, the late Mountainist member of the Convention, and president of the Committee of General Security during the Terror. He was naturally an object of special hatred to the Reaction ; and although he was residing in Toulouse at the time of the Babeuf conspiracy in Paris, and had no connection whatever with the movement, the opportunity was too good to be let slip by his enemies, so the unfortunate old man was dragged from Toulouse to the capital, and thence to Vendôme, to stand his trial before the special high court for a matter of which he knew nothing. But that was not all. So incensed were the authorities against him that he was not allowed to speak even in his own defence. Notwithstanding this, the evidence against him being practically nil, the jury acquitted him without hesitation. Nettled by this failure, and not to be baulked of their prey, the court ordered him to be kept in arrest on the strength of an alleged decree of the Convention for the deportation of certain members of the Mountain, which had since been rescinded. He remained in prison till the Coup d'État of the 18th of Brumaire.

The five prisoners who were convicted of participation in the attempt to re-establish the Constitution of '93, but were given the benefit of extenuating circumstances, were shortly after their conviction interned, together with the acquitted Vadier, in the fortress on the island of Pelée, situated at the entrance to the harbour of Cherbourg. The whole of the way thither they were kept chained and confined in iron cages, exposed in many cases to the insults and threats of reactionary crowds, though towns were not wanting through which they passed where they were received with the most friendly greetings. At Saint Lô, for example, the mayor, at the head of the municipal council, received them with every cordiality as "our unfortunate brothers." In a speech, he declared them to have defended the rights of the people in a manner for which every good citizen owed them gratitude and love.

It may be interesting to follow the career of some of the actors in the events we have been describing. Rèal, the chief counsel for the defence in the Vendôme trial, whose zeal and energy in the performance of his duties on this occasion are not to be gainsaid—notwithstanding that Babeuf, more anxious to affirm his principles than to get off by the denial of the truth, or even on technical grounds, was certainly a difficult client to deal with from the advocate's point of view—this same Rèal became, under the Empire, Prefect of Police, then Councillor of State, and finally Count.   Germain died in 1830, a prosperous agriculturalist, having long deserted the fields of politics.   Drouet, the postmaster of St Menehould, and strenuous member of the Mountain in the Convention, also took service under the the Napoleonic régime, when he became sub-prefect, after having first been decorated with the Legion of Honour.   The Marquis d'Antonelle, the colleague of Drouet on the Mountain, and a fellow-participator with the other Montagnards in the conspiracy of the Equals, appears, after some years of obscurity, after the Restoration, as a strong partisan of the resuscitated Bourbons.   Vadier died in honourable consistency in exile during the Restoration period.   The time and place of the death of his colleague on the Committee of General Security, Amar, remain in some doubt.   Felix Le Pelletier, who succeeded in escaping imprisonment or transportation, was probably the wealthiest man in the movement, and nobly fulfilled his obligations towards the children of his dead friend. Émile he adopted, while he saw towards the placing of the two younger brothers, Camille and Caius, with an old friend of his, a former member of the Convention.

Subsequently, after he was grown up, Émile joined the Spanish patriots in their struggle for

independence.   Happening to hear, while in
Spain, that Grisel, the traitor, who had delivered
over his father to death and his father's friends
to imprisonment and exile, was also there, he
sought him out and challenged him to a duel.
The duel was one to the death. Émile Babeuf
fought with a reckless bravery and fury. Finally
he struck Grisel a mortal blow, but not before
he himself had received a dangerous wound in
the chest.   This, however, was nothing to him.
He had executed vengeance on the traitor.
He subsequently became a bookseller in Lyons,
where, however, he failed.   Returning to Paris,
he started a journal called the *Nain Jaune*, of
strong Jacobin tendencies.   But this also came to
an untimely end, being seized by the police and
suppressed.   He tried bookselling again in Paris,
but this time also with disastrous financial results.
He then seems to have joined the imperial cause,
and to have associated his fortunes with those of
Napoleon the First.   After the fall of the empire
he emigrated to America, where he died in the
early twenties of the last century.   His brother
Caius was killed in battle during the first invasion of French territory in 1814, while his other
brother Camille committed suicide from the
column Vendôme in the following year, 1815, at
the sight of the Cossacks entering Paris.

Émile Babeuf, it may be noted, had one son,

Louis Pierre Babeuf, who occupied various official posts, having been sub-prefect in 1848, inspector of insurances, etc. He died in Paris, 20th February 1871, at the age of sixty-two. With the death of this solitary grandchild of Gracchus Babeuf the name itself became extinct.

The appreciation of his father from the pen of Émile Babeuf, discovered among his papers by M. Victor Advielle, and reproduced by him in his *Histoire de Gracchus Babeuf et du Babouvisme* (vol. i. pp. 344–5) may be of interest :—

"As to the conduct of my father, this belongs to history ; and the facts, however we may regard them, prove nothing against his heart. He may have erred in his actions, but his conscience was never compromised. I will go farther and venture the assurance that he always had pure and disinterested intentions, that he only valued life in so far as he believed it useful to his country, and that he perished, a victim of his opinions, with the same fervour that the saints walked to their martyrdom. I have only one trait to cite that cannot be made public, but which will decide your opinion. Long persecutions by private enemies caused my father to languish in prison till the 9th Thermidor. He cleared himself completely of an accusation of forgery, and was given back to society. But his fortune having been reduced to nothing, in order to obtain food for our little family we were obliged to sell part of our furniture, for at that time famine reigned in Paris. My father was then again thrown into prison. The 13th of Vendémiaire liberated him again, and he continued his journal, entitled the *Tribun du Peuple*. The government then deputed a man to go and see him, whose merits would be sufficiently proved did I but mention his name, in order to persuade him, like Fréron, to exchange his character, his conscience, his pen, for the ministry of finance! My father was revolted at the proposal and broke with the negotiation. No person has hitherto related the fact that at the time of the entry of the Prussians into the plains of Champagne, my father, sent as commissioner of the department of the Somme to Peronne to see to the fortification of the place, defeated a conspiracy there, which aimed at nothing less than delivering the place over to the enemy. He had the guilty arrested, and saved the town from being surprised the following night by an advanced guard of the Prussian army. Finally, no one has told how Paris, notwithstanding neglect and the Maximum, owed its subsistence during eighteen months to the unremitting energies of the general secretary of the Administration of Subsistence, Babeuf, who passed nearly all his nights in working and in distributing their respective tasks to twenty-four employés."

We have no means of testing the truth of the statements contained in the foregoing notice, with the exception of that respecting his work at the victualling commission in Paris, the conscientious thoroughness of which is otherwise confirmed. More especially, as regards the alleged attempt on the part of the government to corrupt Babeuf by means of its mysterious emissary, we are left utterly in the dark, even by Émile himself, as to the nature of the position alleged to have been offered his father in the ministry of finance. But the notice, so far as Émile is concerned, certainly tends to confirm, what we gather from other indications in his career, namely, that with all his political worthlessness and general instability of character, Émile Babeuf always retained an affectionate regard for the memory of his father. In view of this fact, we would willingly believe that his turning his back on the principles in which he had been brought up, and which he himself so ardently championed earlier in his life, in order to cringe before the "Corsican adventurer," was due to this weakness of character, acted on by stress of private circumstances, rather than to any intrinsic moral baseness.

CONCLUSION

THE movement of Babeuf for resuscitating the Revolutionary Government on an economic basis of a Socialist character was a failure, and, like all failures, like all movements that are suppressed with real success, or that, to speak in expressive slang, "peter out," leaving but slight direct traces behind them, has tended with the lapse of years to pass into historical oblivion. Comparatively few men of average education in the present day have ever heard of Babeuf. For the great world, as above said, he left nothing behind him, scarcely even a memory, except for the few interested in the byways and *cul-de-sacs* of history, and who honour single-minded devotion to the popular cause, even when it has been without result.

Of the absolute sincerity, earnestness, and courage of the protagonist of the Equals there can be no sort of doubt with anyone who has studied the history of Babeuf and his ill-starred movement. Of his grasp of the situation, and of his intellectual capacity as the leader of a party of wide-reaching revolutionary aims, as much cannot be said. With all our admiration of Babeuf's energy and heroism as a revolutionary figure, it is impossible to avoid the conclusion that he was intellectually unstable. The correspondence with Dubois de Fosseux and others in his early days already indicated that. We fail to find, moreover, much trace (though we do some) of real originality in the doctrines, into the attempted realisation of which Babeuf threw such unsurpassed energy and self-devotion. They are mainly discoverable in other writers of eighteenth-century France, notably in Morelly, in Mably, and even in Rousseau. Babeuf himself admitted this, protesting that his trial was an attack on the liberty of the press, and that he was being prosecuted for professing doctrines that had had the support of Rousseau, of Mably, and—true eighteenth-century touch—of Lycurgus!

His instability of mind is crucially exhibited in the complete *volte face* he made as regards the question of Robespierre and Thermidor. In his *Journal de la liberté de la presse*, notably in the earlier numbers, we are confronted with measureless denunciations of Robespierre and the Terror, for which he was held responsible. In a short time, as we have seen in an earlier chapter of the present work, this uncompromising attitude became modified in the sense of recognising two Robespierres,—Robespierre, the tyrant of the latter days of the Terror; and Robespierre of earlier days, the sincere apostle of Equality and the Revolution. But the matter did not rest here. Before the end of his political career, Babeuf had come to idolise the late dictator as something like a heaven-sent Messiah of the new era of revolutionary social construction. So far did he go in this, that in a copy of a letter addressed to Joseph Bodson (? Dobson), who appears to have been a Hébertist, found among the papers seized in Babeuf's house, we find the declaration that the Babouvists were but the "second Gracchi" of the French Revolution, the first being Robespierre and his followers. Defending Robespierre against the attacks of his correspondent, "Let us give him back," says he, "his first legitimate glory, and all his disciples would arise anew and soon would triumph. Robespierrism overthrows anew all the factions; Robespierrism does not resemble any of them, it is neither artificial nor limited. Hébertism exists only in Paris and among a small section of men, and can only sustain itself with difficulty. Robespierrism exists throughout the Republic in the whole class of the judicial and clear-sighted, and, of course, among all the people. The reason is simple: it is that Robespierrism is Democracy, and that the two words are identical. Hence, in resuscitating Robespierrism you are sure to resuscitate democracy."

One cannot but regret to find a man like Babeuf singing the praises of the author of the law of Prairial, and the judicial murderer of Anacharsis Clootz and of Chaumette, not to speak of his former friends and colleagues the Dantonists. Babeuf's correspondent replied, warning him of the danger of his hero worship as likely to prejudice his own movement, in view of the name Robespierre had left behind in connection with the Terror, while at the same time repudiating any blind partisanship with the party of Hébert. It is indeed by no means improbable that the injudicious utterances of Babeuf and his exaltation of Robespierre and the Terror did alienate from his movement many of the rank and file of the Paris populace, who, although strong in their revolutionary principles and zealous for the Constitution of '93, had no wish for a return to the pre-Thermidorean revolutionary government, with its Terror "the order of the day." Certainly, before and after the trial the Directorial government used the bogey of a return of the Terror to prejudice the movement of the Babouvists, and not without success among all classes of the population.

It was, moreover, not true that the distinctive feature in the doctrine of Babeuf, its communistic character, was to be found in any of the writings and speeches of Robespierre and his partisans. Robespierre, St Just, and the rest were jealous

upholders of the rights of private property. Their
ideal was a Republic of the small middle-class,
with the citizens possessed each of moderate means,
sober, frugal, laborious, misery and want unknown,
and an accumulation of wealth beyond a certain
limit discouraged. This was the Rousseauite ideal
of the period. Thus, though not possessed of a high
originality, Babeuf certainly does himself injustice
in professing to regard himself as a mere follower
of Robespierre or any other of the earlier leaders.
Probably the Hébertists approached, at least in
spirit, as nearly the standpoint of Babeuf as any of
his predecessors, but even they did not distinctly
formulate any communistic proposals; while Hébert
himself, when on one occasion taunted by Robespierre, at the Jacobin Club, as to heresies on the
subject of private property, the inviolability of
which formed one of the points in the Declaration
of the Rights of Man, expressly repudiated any
such.

The common Rousseauite atmosphere of thought
and phraseology, with denunciations of a society
admitting the extremes of excessive wealth and
indigence, are to be found in all the men of that
time, in Babeuf no less than in the rest. But,
as already said, the remedy proposed by Babeuf
—the notion that only the abolition of the institution of private property itself could cure the
evils of society and prevent their return — was

certainly, as a practical proposal entering the domain of current politics, peculiar to Babeuf. That the communistic idea itself was not original with Babeuf we have already shown in an earlier chapter of the present work. He undoubtedly derived it from the writings of Mably and Morelly. What was original in Babeuf was his attempt to place it as the immediate goal of the society of his time, to be directly realised by political methods. Babeuf was the first to conceive of Communism in any shape as a politically realisable ideal in the immediate or near future.

Before Babeuf there were not wanting indications of what might be termed a Socialist tendency in individual revolutionists, notwithstanding the Convention, as a whole, on the first day of its assembly, had passed a resolution repudiating such tendencies, and decreeing the sacredness of private property. These tendencies were always sporadic in character, but are interesting for what they are worth. Curiously enough, it was the Girondin, Rabaut St Etienne, with whom some of the strongest expressions of opinion in this sense are to be found. Thus, in the *Chronique de Paris* of January 19th, 1793, he demands what he terms a supplement to the political revolution. " With the establishment of political equality," he observes, " the poor soon become sensible that the inequality of fortune vitiates equality ; and inasmuch as equality means independence, they wax bitter and indignant against those on whom they have to depend for their needs. They demand equality of fortune, but it is seldom that the rich are readily disposed to recognise the justice of this claim. Hence it must be obtained either by force or by law." After expressing the fear that force might tend to produce a new inequality, he proceeds to insist on the necessity of laws to effect the more equal division of property ; and not only so, but to maintain this greater equality of wealth when once effected, and to prevent the old inequality from reasserting itself. He goes on to talk, in the Rousseauite fashion of the time, of education in sobriety, modesty, and temperance by means of "moral institutions," among which "institutions" he instances civic feasts, in which all Frenchmen should mingle together, irrespective of wealth or status. He advocates the enactment of laws limiting the amount of fortune a man may possess ; and ordaining that once this maximum is exceeded, society shall step in and take possession of all that is above it.

The article in question, as might be expected, did not pass without adverse criticism, but Rabaut stuck to his guns, and a few days later replied, reaffirming his position. Society, he insists, in according its protection to the individual, has a right, in the last resort, of disposing of the goods of the individual. We need scarcely say that these views of Rabaut

St Etienne did not meet with any sympathy on the part of his colleagues of the Girondin party.

While Rabaut St Etienne was promulgating the above views, an obscure journalist and popular orator named Varlet was also demanding, while admitting the sacredness of private property so long as not abused to the detriment of society, the confiscation by the State of all wealth acquired by monopoly, the rigging of markets, or dishonest speculation. Marat, as we all know, wrote in a similar sense regarding the facts of destitution, as absolving the destitute from all obligations to the society which admitted of it. His celebrated articles against the forestallers were an application of this line of thought. In Marat's writings, in fact, there are distinct indications of attempts at constructive legislative schemes implying far-reaching economic changes, but they remain merely hints. Hébert, again, is strong on the right of the people to make the "wealthy swine, who wax fat on the blood of the poor, to disgorge"; on the duty of the State to confiscate, presumably for redistribution among the indigent, of excessive wealth, which, as he maintains, cannot be acquired by honest means— wealth that only conduced to "needless luxury, worthless display, riding in carriages," etc. But, while urging this, he none the less insists that the notion of perfect equality of fortune is a chimera. In Hébert no more than in the rest do we find

communism in the literal sense of the word.   The
nationalisation, with a view to subsequent division,
of the property of the clergy and emigrant nobles,
had familiarised the people's minds generally with
the idea of confiscation, and had correspondingly
weakened the sentiment of the absoluteness of the
rights of property as such.

But with all this, we look in vain for any definite
socialist or communist formulation of policy.   The
utmost we find in these revolutionary writers is the
notion of the dividing up of the land (an agrarian
law), and possibly of the products of consumption,
and this most of them rejected as impracticable and
utopian.   The prevailing state of industry and the
economic conditions generally of the eighteenth
century were not yet sufficiently advanced for the
idea of the common ownership and co-operative
working, in the common interest, of the means of
production, to take definite shape.

Hence the average mind of the eighteenth
century could never get beyond the notion, as
regards social reconstruction, of the repartition of
the land and of the products of industry, as being
the starting-point and the central principle of all
such reconstruction.

Babeuf himself did not see so much beyond
his contemporaries in this matter, but, at all
events, he proclaimed communism as the essential
of social regeneration, and he had some idea of

the organisation of productive labour in common. As with the rest, he regarded the means towards the regeneration of human nature to consist, in the main, in a system of education. This system of educational direction was to continue through-out life. To quote the words of a manifesto by Babeuf's Insurrectionary Committee: "In the social order conceived by the committee, the country (*i.e.* the State) shall seize upon the new-born individual, never to leave him till his death. It shall watch over his first moments, shall assure the milk and the care of her who gave him birth, shall guard him from all that might injure his health and enervate his body, shall shield him from a false tenderness, and shall take him, by the hand of his mother, to the national home (*maison nationale*), where he shall acquire virtue and the illumination necessary to a true citizen."

The ideal life of the individual appears to Babeuf, as to others of his contemporaries, to involve to a large extent severity and frugality of living—always the ideal of the peasant and the small independent craftsman. All is to be excluded that is not necessary to republican virtue; "a rustic simpli-city" should take the place of elegance of furniture and of garments. In short, Babeuf's scheme bears upon it the unmistakable impress of his day and generation. As before said, what distinguishes Babeuf from his revolutionary predecessors is his

placing communism, involving the definite abolition
of the institution of private property, in the fore-
front of his doctrine, in the more definite character
of the latter, and in his bold idea of its prompt
realisation by political means, through a committee
of select persons placed in power by the people's
will as the issue of a popular insurrection. In
illustration of this may be quoted a passage from
the manifesto of the Equals relative to the agrarian
law, by which was understood partition of the
soil among the peasant cultivators, and which was
regarded as the extreme limit of economic revolution. " We aim at," says the manifesto, " something more sublime and more just than this—the
common good or the community of goods ; no more
individual property in land ; the land belongs to
no one. We claim, we demand the common enjoyment of the fruits of the earth. These fruits
belong to the whole world."

The delusion that Robespierre was essentially
a man of the people rather than of the middle
bourgeoisie is sufficiently disposed of when we
consider the measures of Robespierre's government
in the second Committee of Public Safety, which
lasted a year. It is true that, in view of the
famine in Paris, it got passed the Decree of September 1793, by which forty sous a day were
granted to those attending the assemblies of the
sections. By these means it put an end, for the

time being, to the rioting which had been going on for a long time almost continuously in Paris. But this was little more than a sop thrown to Cerberus. It was necessary to ward off the danger of another organised insurrection. On the other hand, the Committee of Public Safety enacted severe regulations against workmen's combinations or assemblies with a view of raising wages or otherwise affecting trade interests. Those, indeed, who should complain, in the State factories now established for the manufacture of arms and munitions of war, were threatened with ferocious penalties. All parties, including Robespierre and his friends, were eloquent in generalities respecting the desirability of a greater equality in incomes, condemning the existence side by side in the same society of abject indigence on the one side and overweening luxury on the other. But these, for the most part, were, as we have seen, mere repetitions of phrases common at the time. Those who, like the Hébertists, really desired to bring about greater economic equality, soon found themselves denounced by Robespierre and his friends as *enragés*, and ultimately sent to the guillotine for their pains.

Towards the end of his political career, indeed, when Robespierre was desirous of conciliating the European powers, and still more the wealthier *bourgeoisie* at home, he became more emphatic than ever

17

in denouncing all attacks on the principle of private property. Babeuf's later obsession in favour of Robespierre, which went so far, as we have seen, as to proclaim him the protagonist of his own ideas, can only be explained by his hatred of the Thermidoreans, who had supplanted Robespierre and the party he represented; although certain Robespierrists with whom he came into close contact, especially the Lebon family in Arras, and probably, more than all, his colleague and fellow-martyr, Darthé, may well have had not inconsiderable influence on his change of view. The change between the Babeuf of the *Journal de la liberté de la presse* and of the *Système de dépopulation*, and the Babeuf of the later numbers of the *Tribun du Peuple*, is indeed remarkable. We may, indeed, take it as indicating a certain weakness in Babeuf's character; but if so, it was weakness that indicated an ingenuousness of disposition. The founder of the movement of the Equals, we can readily see, was possessed of an emotional temperament which carried him away, quite regardless of personal considerations. That he was prepared to shelter his own reputation for originality, without cause or justification, behind that of Robespierre, certainly indicates an absence of personal vanity not a little unusual in the founders of popular movements.

Babeuf's mind was undoubtedly more original than Robespierre's, although the latter had what

Babeuf lacked. Robespierre's ideas, as ideas, were but a pale reflex of the teachings of Rousseau. The success of Robespierre was due to his consistent pertinacity in urging them, and to his capacity for imbuing his colleagues and the Paris populace with the notion that he was the pure and disinterested personification of those ideas. Babeuf had little of Robespierre's dexterity ; but his boldness in applying, not only the revolutionary side of Rousseau's teachings, but the Utopian theories of Mably and Morelly to the France of his day ; his idea of seizing the political power by a *coup de main*, with a view to the immediate reorganisation of society on a communist basis, was in itself original in its inception. More than this we do not claim for Babeuf on the score of originality.

In any case, Gracchus Babeuf and his movement cannot fail to be for the modern socialist of the deepest possible historical interest. Gracchus Babeuf was, in a sense, a pioneer and a hero of the modern international Socialist party.

The movement of Babeuf had a kind of aftermath in the nineteenth century in that of Auguste Blanqui. The Blanquist notion of the seizure of the political power by a *coup de main* on the part of a revolutionary minority, as the sole effective method preliminary to the reorganisation of society, is clearly traceable to the movement of the Equals, and the projected insurrection of the year V. Born on the 7th of February 1805, only eight years after the execution of Babeuf, son of a member of the Convention, Blanqui in his early youth came into direct contact with the old revolutionary tradition, and possibly had personal acquaintance with survivors of the Babouvists' movement. He was certainly well read in the old revolutionary literature. His influence on all the revolutionary movements of France during the nineteenth century was immense, and his following considerable among the student class, especially in Paris, during the early and mid-nineteenth century, as well as with the working classes of the large towns. Auguste Blanqui is a monumental instance of single-minded devotion to an ideal absolutely regardless of self, not in a time of crisis merely, but throughout a long life, for this noble old man closed his career of unflinching devotion, which included thirty-seven years of imprisonment, in 1881, at the age of seventy-six. Two sayings of his may be quoted, as affording good instances of the influence of Babeuf and his doctrines on the nineteenth century revolutionary movements. In summing up his position on one occasion Blanqui wrote: "The social question cannot be earnestly and effectively discussed till after the next energetic and irrevocable solution of the political question." And again, in a programme drawn up by him in 1869, we read: "The day after the Revolution, when the nation sees a new horizon before it, two parallel paths must be followed : the one leads to education, the other to the co-operation of the productive forces towards a common end." We see here plainly enough how the traditions of the movement of 1796 were carried down by a powerful personality far into the nineteenth century. And the influence of Blanqui still lives. Although the actual reconstructive proposals of Babeuf, and hence Babouvism as a Social doctrine, may be dead and superseded to-day, yet the Blanquists' notion, derived from the Babouvists, of the seizure of the political power by the revolutionary act of a minority, and the superintendence of the work of reconstruction by that minority, has still a following in the modern Socialist party.

INDEX